9500

PERSIAN GLASS

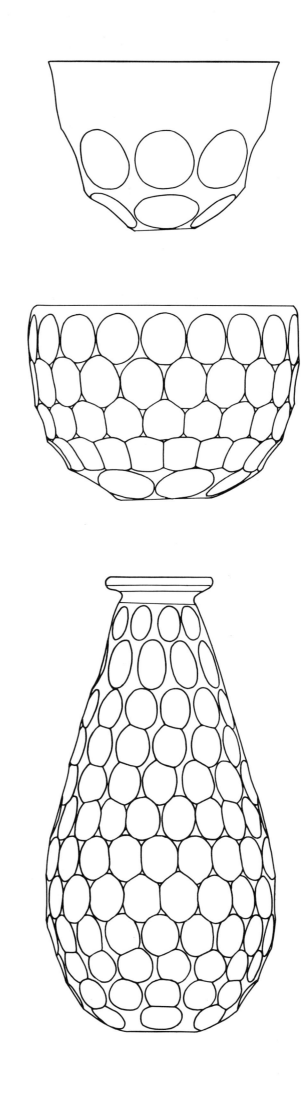

SHINJI FUKAI

PERSIAN GLASS

translated by

Edna B. Crawford

with photographs by

Bin Takahashi

WEATHERHILL/TANKOSHA
New York, Tokyo, Kyoto

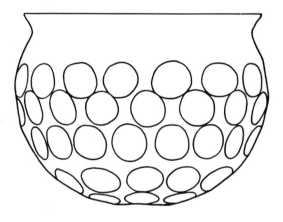

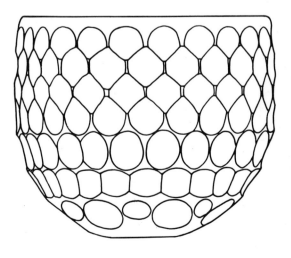

This book was originally published in Japanese by Tankosha in 1973 under the title *Perushia no Garasu* (Persian Glass).

First English edition, 1977

Published jointly by John Weatherhill, Inc., of New York and Tokyo, with editorial offices at 7-6-13 Roppongi, Minato-ku, Tokyo 106; and Tankosha, Kyoto. Copyright © 1973, 1977, by Tankosha; all rights reserved. Printed in Japan.

Library of Congress Cataloging in Publication Data: Fukai, Shinji, 1924– / Persian glass. / Translation of Perushia no garasu. / 1. Glassware—Iran. 2. Iran—Antiquities. / I. Takahashi, Bin. II. Title. / NK5174.A1F8413 / 1977 / 748.5′9955 / 77-23736 / ISBN 0-8348-1515-x

Contents

Forewords

I have no scholarly knowledge of glass; I am simply a layman who cries admiringly "How beautiful!" whenever he sees fine ancient or modern works in glass. Paintings and ceramics are also beautiful, of course, but because I sense a certain romance in glass objects, I am especially drawn to them.

However, Professor Shinji Fukai's *Study of Iranian Art and Archaeology: Glassware and Metalware*, published in 1968, aroused my scholarly interest as well. When I was a research student in the Faculty of Letters of Tokyo University, Professor Fukai, who was on the staff of the university's art history research institute, was one of my instructors. In 1956, while visiting excavations by the Tokyo University Iraq-Iran Archaeological Expedition at Telul-eth Thalathat in northern Iraq, I met Professor Fukai again and had an opportunity to observe his work first hand. This expedition stimulated his enthusiasm for the study of the arts of the ancient Middle East.

Professor Fukai has since continued his research in this area. His discovery and subsequent acquisition of a glass bowl with circular facets, of the same type as the glass bowl in the Shōsō-in of Nara, Japan, at an antique shop in Teheran in 1959 is especially noteworthy. Until then, the striking similarities between ancient Persian glass bowls and the one in the Shōsō-in had not been noted even in Iran. Professor Fukai's research and papers on this subject created a stir in the academic world, both in Japan and in Iran. Thus the fact of cultural contact between Japan and Persia in ancient times via the Silk Road was dramatically underscored.

Professor Fukai's study of Persian glass has culminated in the publication of this superb book. The text presents a history of Persian glassware, focusing on that of the Sassanian dynasty (226–642), which had such a great influence on Japanese culture during the Nara period (646–794). The book also contains beautiful color photographs by Mr. Bin Takahashi. I believe readers will find this book of the greatest interest.

H.I.H. PRINCE TAKAHITO MIKASA

Until now, no introductory work on Persian glass from the early first millennium B.C. into the Islamic period has been available either in Japan or elsewhere. Professor Fukai's book offers a general survey of this subject, concentrating on the Partho-Sassanian period (249 B.C.–A.D. 642), with detailed commentary on style, design, technique, and artistic value, as well as illustrations of representative pieces. I think it unlikely that anyone but Professor Fukai could have written this kind of comprehensive introduction to Persian glass. Prior to World War II it was not even clear that there *was* such a thing as ancient Persian glass. Japanese scholars had conjectured from their reading of Chinese sources and from studying the treasures in the Shōsō-in that the glass bowl and carafe preserved there since the eighth century had been brought to Japan from China but had originated in Persia or elsewhere in the Middle East. However, it was not known whether glass objects that could corroborate this hypothesis actually existed in Iran today.

When diplomatic relations between Japan and Iran were reestablished after World War II and cultural exchange between the two nations resumed, it was Professor Fukai who first noticed, in the Teheran Archaeological Museum, a glass vessel from Persia's Sassanian dynasty that was strikingly similar to the glass carafe in the Shōsō-in. Here was the first concrete evidence linking ancient Persia and Japan. Encouraged, Professor Fukai investigated further and found that not only glass carafes but also glass bowls were being offered on Teheran's antique market as pieces from Amlash in Gilan Province in the Iranian highlands. This occurred in March of 1959.

This discovery triggered considerable research on Persian glass vessels. In 1960 the Tokyo University Iraq-Iran Archaeological Expedition began excavating ancient tombs in Dailaman, Gilan Province, searching for the sites where the objects had actually been found. The expedition did find various glass vessels among the burial goods unearthed. Naturally Professor Fukai, a member of the expedition, took charge of the study of the glassware that was found, and later published several reports that drew attention in the academic world both in Japan and overseas.

Stimulated by these excavations, an expedition from the University of Teheran proceeded to excavate groups of tombs in Marlik, Gilan Province. Among the finds was a very beautiful and unusual glass vessel. Using as criteria various ancient Persian glass objects found in the course of scientific excavations and dating from the early first millennium B.C. to the Partho-Sassanian period, it became possible for the first time to carry out research on Persian glass objects that had been found, or in some cases had been preserved for centuries, outside Iran—in Russia, Western Europe, and Japan.

The availability of comparative materials from Japan increased when fragments of glass vessels recognized as Persian in origin were found in Japan, in a religious mound on the island of Okino-shima off Kyushu and in the Kamigamo district of Kyoto. In addition, a glass bowl had been found earlier in the tumulus of the Japanese emperor Ankan (r. 531–35) in Osaka Prefecture. Professor Fukai examined all these materials and made a comprehensive study of the subject. He has also carried out research on Persian glass of the Islamic period, and in this book presents a general view of Persian glass of all periods. From the standpoint of both materials and research, I believe, no one else could have accomplished this.

I am delighted at the publication of this excellent book. Combined with Mr. Takahashi's vivid photographs, Professor Fukai's text makes this the first truly introductory work on Persian glass. I can recommend it with confidence.

NAMIO EGAMI
Professor Emeritus, Tokyo University

Preface

That the Japanese today immediately associate the words "Persian glass" with well-known examples of Persian glassware preserved for centuries in Japan, such as the bowl and carafe in the Shōsō-in and the bowl from the tumulus of Emperor Ankan, is due largely to recent archaeological excavations in the Middle East that have clarified the nature and indeed the very existence of ancient glass in Persia. In books published before World War II, one finds, the discussion of Persian glass is restricted to works of the Islamic period, beginning in the seventh to eighth century. The existence of pre-Islamic glass was unknown except for the artifacts excavated at Gurgan in northern Iran.

Since 1958, however, several groups of tombs dating to the Parthian and Sassanian dynasties of Persia have been discovered in the Elburz Mountains in Gilan Province, in the northern Iranian highlands. The numerous glass objects unearthed, whose existence had previously been unsuspected, show clearly that Persian culture of the Parthian and Sassanian dynasties played a vital role in East-West cultural exchange, as seen in the similarity of these works to others found in locations ranging from Germany to Japan.

Perhaps because it was easy for Japanese investigators to see the close relationship between Persian art of this period and numerous objects preserved in the Shōsō-in, many works found in Gilan, including glassware, have come into the possession of Japanese museums and collectors over the past ten years or so. We believe the time is right to present to the general public a survey of Persian glass, illustrated by works of the Partho-Sassanian period that are now in Japan. We hope thus to deepen understanding of the aesthetic and historical value of ancient Persian glass. Fortunately, Japanese collectors have been most cooperative.

Finally, we would like to express our deep gratitude to His Imperial Highness Prince Takahito Mikasa, Honorary President of the Society for Near Eastern Studies in Japan, and to Namio Egami, Professor Emeritus of Tokyo University, for contributing forewords. We also thank all who have assisted us in the preparation and publication of this book.

SHINJI FUKAI
BIN TAKAHASHI

11

PERSIAN GLASS

1 Early Glass

From Prehistoric Times to the Achaemenid Dynasty

The Khuzistan region of the southwestern Iranian highlands, adjoining southern Mesopotamia, very early came under the influence of Mesopotamian culture. Glass made from vitreous glazes, which were known by 4000 B.C., apparently appeared around 3000 B.C. in both Mesopotamia and Egypt. Glass has not been found in the ruins of farming settlements of this early time in the Iranian highlands. However, early in the second millennium B.C., when most of the Iranian highlands were still in a preliterate state, the kingdom of Elam, centered on Susa, emerged; here a high level of culture flourished, and glass was used.

ELAM   Forty kilometers southeast of Susa are the ruins known as Tchoga Zanbil. Here a ziggurat was built by King Untashgal (r. c. 1265–1245 B.C.) in the Middle Elamite period. These ruins, discovered in 1935, have been systematically excavated by the French archaeological expeditions led by Dr. Roman Ghirshman, and restoration of the ziggurat is now complete. Numerous cylinder seals of the Middle Elamite period have been found on the site of the worship hall attached to the ziggurat.[1] Among these seals, carved with Kassite and Elamite designs, are a number made of dark blue glass. Similar cylinder seals have been found at Susa (fig.1). All these glass cylinder seals must have been made in Elam.

1. Glass cylinder seal
from Tchoga Zanbil

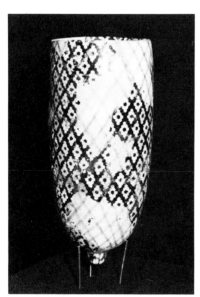

2. Situla-shaped glass vessel
from Marlik

Why did glass suddenly come into use as a material for cylinder seals at this time? At present, the most reasonable explanation is connected with lapis lazuli.[2] In the ancient Middle East, particularly in northern Mesopotamia, the blue, purplish blue, or greenish blue beauty of lapis lazuli was highly prized. Lapis lazuli became the favorite material for jewelry and other ornaments around 3500 B.C. It is believed that this lapis lazuli came from the Badakhshan region of northeastern Afghanistan, clearly indicating that there was trade at that time between Badakhshan and Mesopotamia, 2,400 kilometers apart. The trade route led from Tepe Sialk through Tepe Hissar in the northeastern Iranian highlands, then through Tepe Giyan to northern Mesopotamia. It was not until after the Jemdet Nasr period (around 3000 B.C.) that lapis lazuli appeared in southern Mesopotamia. It seems to have been imported from Tepe Sialk through Susa in Elam, and probably was also exported by sea from Susa to Egypt.[3]

The Elamites must also have been active as intermediaries for Sumerian importation of lapis lazuli until around the thirteenth century B.C., when suddenly the use of dark blue glass began to replace lapis lazuli as the material for cylinder seals. This change was unquestionably due to the influence of either Mesopotamia or Egypt, where glass had long been known.

Since World War II extensive archaeological excavations have been carried out in the Iranian highlands. In Gilan Province in the northern highlands and Azerbaijan in the northwestern highlands, regions previously neglected, many burial mounds of the late Bronze Age and early Iron Age have been discovered, as well as numerous tombs of the Partho-Sassanian period. Two objects excavated at Marlik in Gilan and fragments of three objects excavated at Hasanlu in the Azerbaijan region are the oldest glass artifacts from this area found so far.

MARLIK   During 1961 and 1962, Dr. Ezat O. Negahban of the University of Teheran excavated excellently preserved artifacts of the late Bronze Age at Marlik on the outskirts of Rudbar in Gilan.[4] These included pottery figurines, gold and silver vessels, miniature bronze animals, and weapons. Among the finds were two glass vessels, described below, made by the so-called mosaic technique of bonding glass rods of different colors.

1. *A situla-shaped vessel.* Approximately 1200–1000 B.C. (Teheran Archaeological Museum, no. 14696; fig. 2). The surface of this vessel is covered with a rosette-in-lozenge design. The lozenge pattern is achieved by bonding nine rods of glass in the mosaic technique, each lozenge consisting of alternating pieces of white and blue glass, with a piece of red glass in the center. The areas between the lozenges are filled with red glass, which apparently functions as a binder, as does the

piece of red glass in the center of each lozenge. Many situla-shaped vessels with buttonlike ornaments at the base, and dating from the middle or late second millennium B.C., have been excavated, mainly at Nuzi and Assur in northern Mesopotamia and also at Alalakh in northern Syria. Examples of the same kind of vessel have also been found among the bronzes from Luristan in the western Iranian highlands. The oldest examples of glass vessels made by the mosaic technique have been discovered among the artifacts excavated from the ruins at Tell el Rimach (approximately 1500 B.C.) in northern Mesopotamia and at Aqar Quf (approximately 1400 B.C.) in central Mesopotamia. It has been suggested that the beginnings of this method may be traced to the mosaic-style wall decorations in the ruins of the ancient Sumerian city of Uruk (or Erech) dating to the late fourth millennium B.C.[5]

2. *A beaker-shaped vessel*. Early first millennium B.C. (Teheran Archaeological Museum, no. 14719; fig. 3). This vessel's pattern of horizontal stripes is created by intertwining thin glass strings or filaments of two different colors (red and white, white and blue, blue and yellow) like a net, then piling one "net" on top of another. Two ribbonlike horizontal bands (blue, white, blue) divide the design into three distinct areas. The lip is trimmed with a blue glass band; the base, also of blue glass, is flat. The technique of using two intertwined strings of different-colored glass originated in Egypt much earlier than the first millennium B.C. It is also seen in the core-molded glass of a later period found in Mesopotamia.

HASANLU   Since World War II fragments of mosaic glass have been excavated at the Hasanlu ruins south of Lake Rezaiyeh in the northwestern Iranian highlands. According to Professor Robert H. Dyson's chronology, they were found in the ruins of the burned building II, which belongs to the fourth Hasanlu period (around the second half of the ninth century B.C.).

Nine fragments of this mosaic glass are presumed to have come from the same vessel. Reconstructed, it is beaker-shaped, the body tapering toward the base. The mosaic design on the body is divided horizontally into two areas. The upper portion probably represents four or five men in procession, while the lower portion depicts crouching goats and a palmette motif. The colors used in the mosaic are red, white, and two shades of blue, ultramarine and dark blue. The height of the vessel is estimated to have been 16 cm.[6]

Several other pieces of mosaic glass similar in design and technique, and presumed to be parts of two other beakers, have also been excavated. All these mosaic-glass objects exhibit Mesopotamian elements (for example, the men depicted on the beaker-shaped vessel described above are obviously Assyrian) and clearly did not originate in the Iranian highlands.

3. Beaker-shaped glass vessel from Marlik

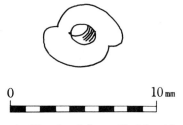

0   10 mm

4. Glass bead from Ghalekuti I

DAILAMAN As mentioned above, since the war numerous burial mounds have been discovered in Gilan Province in the northern Iranian highlands. In 1960 and 1964, archaeological expeditions from Tokyo University excavated groups of tombs dating from the early first millennium B.C. in the Ghalekuti hills of the Dailaman region in the eastern part of the province. Here they found no glass vessels, such as those recovered from Marlik and Hasanlu, but did discover many glass beads. Naturally glass beads were also unearthed at Marlik and Hasanlu, but as no finds of glass beads from prehistoric sites in the Iranian highlauds have previously been published, here I will discuss a few important examples excavated in Dailaman.

A total of forty-one glass beads was found in Ghalekuti tombs I-CI, A-IV, and B-III. According to the report by Sachiko Oda of the National Science Museum of Japan,[7] these include seventeen small beads, eight spherical beads, eight spheroid beads, six inlaid beads, one tangerine-shaped bead, and one square bead. Of these, seventeen beads retain their original glassy quality. Three different colors are found: the eight spherical beads are yellowish green and translucent; the small beads and the inlaid beads are greenish blue and translucent; and the square bead is blue and translucent. The glass inlays are badly eroded and it is difficult to determine the original colors, but in their present condition the inlaid sections are either bright yellow or white and can be distinguished clearly from the background color, indicating an intentional contrast.

Four of the inlaid beads have two or three round pieces inset. The other two beads have an inlay of one or two bands encircling the midsection. One characteristic of these two kinds of inlaid beads is that the inlaid pieces are not raised above the background surface. Another characteristic is the relatively large size of the round inlays in comparison to those seen in inlaid beads of the later Partho-Sassanian period.

These finds establish that inlaid beads were made as early as the first millennium B.C. in the Iranian highlands. The technique used to make small beads is also of interest. Many were fashioned by winding glass strings two or three times around a cylindrical core. Among the small beads excavated were some oddly shaped beads that look like two joined hemispheres that have slipped (fig. 4), a form unique to this early period.

The Achaemenid Dynasty

Whether glass vessels were actually manufactured in the Iranian highlands during the Achaemenid dynasty (550–330 B.C.) is not yet determined. Glass vessels attributed to this period have been found in various parts of the Middle East, including Meso-

5. Reconstructed phiale-shaped glass dish (¼ actual size)

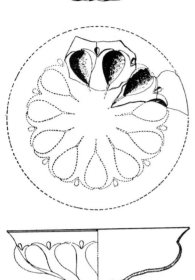

6. Glass dish with lotus design (¼ actual size)

potamia, Anatolia, and Palestine, but not in the Iranian highlands, and the locale of their manufacture is still unknown. All that has been discovered in the Iranian highlands is a few fragments of glass vessels, found when the ruins of the treasury of the palace at Persepolis, in the Fars region of the southern Iranian highlands, were excavated. Only this glassware will be discussed below.

The glass fragments found at Persepolis between 1931 and 1934 by members of the Oriental Institute of the University of Chicago are believed to have originally belonged to twenty-four different objects. Most of them were unearthed from the ruins of the palace treasury, and as it is known that the palace was destroyed by fire in 331 B.C. during the eastern campaign of Alexander the Great, we have at least a terminal date for their manufacture.

The fragments come from a dish, a lid, a water jar, a beaker-shaped vessel, a wine glass, and nineteen other unidentifiable objects. The most important fragments are those of the dish, and it was possible to ascertain the vessel's original shape from its fragments (fig. 5). This is a phiale-shaped dish, a shape also seen in certain contemporary metal vessels. The central portion of the dish bulges outward and bears a raised design of a circular lotus whose petals radiate from the base of the dish. This design is similar to that on an embossed silver dish (fig. 6) bearing the name of King Artaxerxes I of Persia (r. 464–424 B.C.),[8] to cite just one example.

A similar phiale-shaped glass dish in the British Museum (Fig. 7) was excavated from the ruins of the Temple of Artemis at Ephesus in western Asia Minor (modern Turkey). This too was clearly inspired by embossed metalware.

7. Phiale-shaped dish from Ephesus

19

8. Fragment of glass rhyton

According to a 1957 report,[9] not a single fragment of a glass vessel made by the mold-blowing technique was among the fragments found at Persepolis; presumably the vessels were made by pressing lumps of glass into shape. While the report states that these vessels were made during the Achaemenid dynasty, it adds that there are no grounds for assuming that any glass vessels were actually produced in the Iranian highlands during that period. The report concludes that the place of manufacture should be sought somewhere in the lowlands to the west. Poul Fossing thinks that the glass dish found at Ephesus was made in Mesopotamia,[10] while Axel von Saldern considers that the objects from Persepolis were made in western Iran or eastern Iraq.[11] More recently, neither Dan Barag, in a paper on a cut glass bowl of the Achaemenid dynasty found at Nippur in Mesopotamia,[12] nor Andrew Oliver, Jr., writing on glass vessels of the same period,[13] has attempted to specify place of manufacture.

Among glass found recently at Persepolis by excavators from the Iranian Center of Archaeological Research is a fragment of a rhyton (fig. 8). The body has been lost, but the base remains, complete with the depiction in relief of a lion attacking a crouching bull, a study reminiscent of the reliefs at Persepolis illustrating the same theme. The rhyton was made of pale green glass, though what remains has effloresced to a golden color, containing many air bubbles. The eyes of both the bull and the lion were inlaid, but the inlays are gone. The rhyton's form was copied from one used for vessels made of precious metals; shapes unique to glassware had not yet appeared during the Achaemenid dynasty, and copies of shapes used in metalware predominated.

Since the state of glassmaking in the Iranian highlands under the Achaemenid dynasty is still so unclear, the place where these vessels were actually made cannot be determined, but I suspect that it was the Mesopotamian region, not the Iranian highlands.

2 The Partho–Sassanian Period

Under the Parthian dynasty (249 B.C.–A.D. 226), which followed the Achaemenid after a period of Macedonian rule, Persia became a point of contact for Occident and Orient, an intermediary in the traffic and trade between the Roman Empire and China. It was during this period that the route known as the Silk Road was opened.

The Parthians were contemporary with the Han dynasty (206 B.C.–A.D. 220) in China, and the importance of the Parthians is attested by contemporary Chinese records. The section concerning the Parthian dynasty (the *Hsi-yü-chuan*, or ''Commentaries on the Western Region'') in the *Hou-han Shu* (Records of the Later Han) states that Pan Ch'ao, Protector General of the Western Region, sent Kan-yin to find the Roman Empire in A.D. 97, but the envoy was unable to achieve his aim because of interference by the Parthians. In the section on the Roman Empire in the same work, it is noted that the Parthians, as the middlemen between China and Rome, made a fortune from the silk trade. This source further records that the Roman emperor Marcus Aurelius Antoninus (r. 161–80) was able to send an envoy to China for the first time in 166.

The Parthian dynasty, which eventually came fully under the sway of the Hellenism that had entered from the West, was finally overthrown in 226 by Ardashir, who established the Sassanian dynasty (226–642). The Sassanians, who came to power by advocating a return to traditional (that is, Achaemenid) Persian ways, created a distinctive Persian culture that had considerable influence in both the Orient and the Occident. Reaching as far east as Afghanistan, the artistic styles of the Sassanian dynasty influenced and modified the local Buddhist

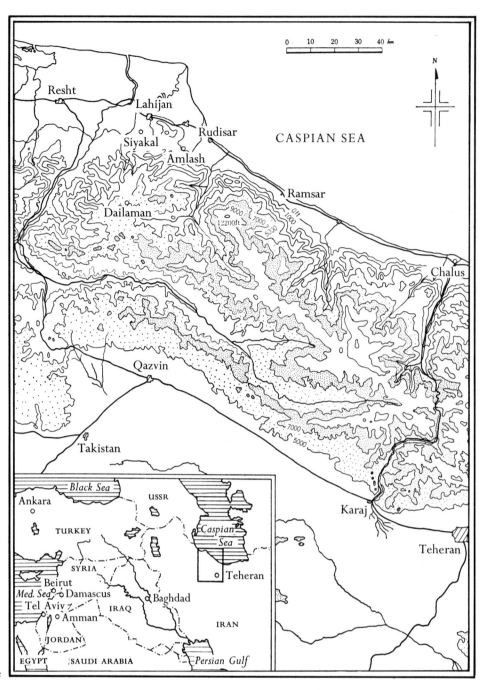

Map labels (reading from the map):

Resht

Lahijan

Rudisar

Siyakal

Amlash

CASPIAN SEA

Ramsar

Dailaman

9000

12200ft 7000

1000

500

Chalus

Qazvin

7000

5000

Takistan

Karaj

Teheran

Black Sea

Ankara

USSR

TURKEY

Caspian Sea

Teheran

SYRIA

Beirut

Med. Sea Damascus

Tel Aviv Baghdad

Amman IRAQ

JORDAN

IRAN

EGYPT SAUDI ARABIA

Persian Gulf

9. Eastern Gilan Province

tradition of Gandharan art, giving rise to the style known as Irano-Buddhist. Persian influence spread even farther east, greatly affecting Buddhist mural art, such as that seen at Kizil on the Silk Road in Central Asia. And in China the Persian style was fashionable from the time of the Six Dynasties (220–589) through the Sui (589–618) and T'ang (618–907) dynasties.

The Persians, who were known to the Chinese as the Hu (literally, "barbarians"), introduced Zoroastrianism, which became very popular in Ch'ang-an, the Chinese capital. Persian culture and manners were also received favorably by the Chinese court and upper classes: Persian food was served, and women favored clothing in the Persian mode.

Persian culture and goods were further transmitted to Japan by embassies sent by the Japanese court to the Sui and T'ang courts. Material evidence of the impact of Persia on Japan can be seen today among the treasures preserved in the Shōsō-in repository of the Tōdai-ji temple in Nara and in the Hōryū-ji temple near Nara.

To return to the Iranian highlands, an epochal archaeological discovery bearing on Persian ancient history was made around 1958. This was the excavation of the so-called Amlash treasure. After World War II the attention of archaeologists concerned with Iran became focused primarily on the northern and northwestern Iranian highlands, which had not yet been excavated. Ziwiyeh in the Azerbaijan region of the northern highlands was excavated in 1947; this was followed by the excavation in 1957 of Hasanlu.

Following upon these great discoveries, beginning in 1958 many groups of tombs from the Partho-Sassanian period, dating from the mid-third century B.C. to the fifth or sixth century A.D., were discovered deep in the Elburz Mountains, which stretch east to west along the southern coast of the Caspian Sea in Gilan Province in the northern highlands of Iran. Numerous glass objects were found in these tombs, arousing great interest among Japanese scholars, who are particularly interested in the history of East-West cultural interchange.

Until these discoveries, the very existence of Partho-Sassanian glass was unknown: when Persian glass was mentioned, it was in reference to the Islamic period. The fact that many glass bowls with circular facets (pl. 1) have been found in Gilan casts light on such questions as the place of manufacture of the glass bowl in the Shōsō-in and of the glass bowl discovered in the tomb of Emperor Ankan (r. 531–35) in Osaka Prefecture. Moreover, artifacts have been discovered in Gilan that are similar to other important objects found in Japan, such as the fragments of a glass bowl with facets in relief found in 1953 on Okinoshima island in the Genkai Sea off Kyushu; the glass bowl with circular facets unearthed in 1963 from the Niizawa Senzuka tombs at Kashiwabara, Nara Prefecture (c. fifth century A.D.); and the fragments of a glass bowl with double circular facets found in 1964 in the Kamigamo district of Kyoto. The finds made in Gilan substantiate the belief that the objects discovered in Japan originated in the Iranian highlands.

Nor is the importance of the glass objects from Gilan limited to the history of the influence of Middle Eastern culture on the ancient civilizations of East Asia in general and of Japan in particular. The discovery in Gilan of Syrian glass, presumably imported, and of works thought to have been made by techniques learned from Syrian glassmaking, in addition to the thick glass bowls unique to the Iranian highlands, is significant for Occidental history, as well. These finds demonstrate that although the Parthian and Sassanian dynasties were continually in political opposition to the Roman world, close cultural relations were always maintained.

Excavation Sites and Conditions of Finds

As already mentioned, beginning in 1958 a number of groups of tombs of the Parthian and Sassanian dynasties were discovered in and around Gilan Province, and a great deal of glassware was unearthed. However, it is very difficult to learn much about the condition of the objects when they were found or the period of their manufacture because in many cases they were dug up by grave robbers, so hardly any scientific evidence is available. Under these circumstances it is virtually impossible to make a distinction between the works of the Parthian and the Sassanian dynasties. As a matter of expediency, therefore, they are described together in this section.

In 1960 and 1964, the Tokyo University Iraq-Iran Archaeological Expedition excavated groups of Partho-Sassanian tombs in Gilan. The excavations centered on the Sefid-rud (Red River) and that part of the province to the east of the Sefid-rud. Special attention was paid to the Dailaman region. A general survey of eastern Gilan was made, and a certain amount of information was obtained, some of it gathered from the local people. This is summarized below.

DAILAMAN   Throughout the Elburz Mountains, which rise in the Pamir knot and run from east to west in the northern Iranian highlands, are to be found clusters of ancient tombs. The regions of Somam, Eshqavar, and Ammarlou contain many burial sites of the late Bronze Age and early Iron Age, while groups of tombs of the Partho-Sassanian period are scattered within the Dailaman and Rahmatabad regions.

Access to the Dailaman region is difficult from both the lowlands along the Caspian Sea to the north of the Elburz Mountains and from the plateau of the Iranian highlands south of these mountains. There are three possible routes. The first is from Rudisar on the Caspian Sea to the hamlet of Omam in the center of the Somam basin, via the town of Amlash at the foot of the Elburz Mountains. From Amlash the traveler proceeds west to the Dailaman valley. (Probably the reason that the artifacts found in Gilan are generally called the "Amlash treasure" is that when the ancient tombs were discovered and dug up by robbers, the objects found were first gathered in Amlash, from where they were taken to Teheran.)

The second route proceeds northwest from Rudisar along the coast to Lahijan via Langerud. From Lahijan the route runs south along the foot of the Elburz Mountains to the town of Siyakal. From there, it is a two-day walk through the great forests and streams of the Elburz foothills, then a climb over a rugged mountain pass to the hamlet of Ispeli in the Dailaman valley. To reach Dailaman itself, one goes south from Ispeli to the Shah-rud, a tributary of the Pul-i-rud.

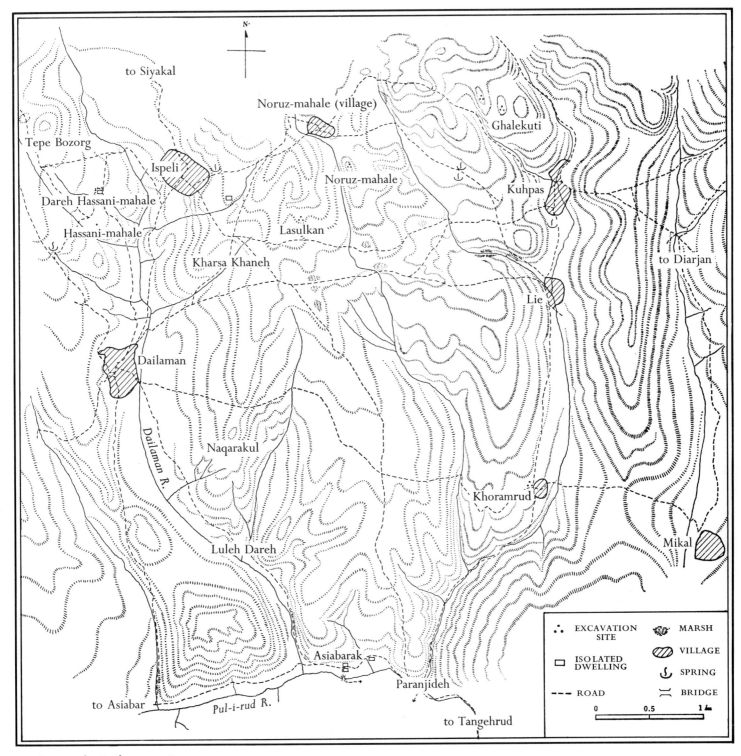

10. Sites in the Dailaman region

The third route to Dailaman is by the main road connecting
Teheran with Resht, the largest city on the Caspian Sea,
via Qazvin. The town of Rudbar lies along this road, which
parallels the Sefid-rud as it flows through the ravines of the
Elburz Mountains into the Caspian Sea. From this town the
Dailaman valley is reached from the west via the hamlet of
Nesfi.

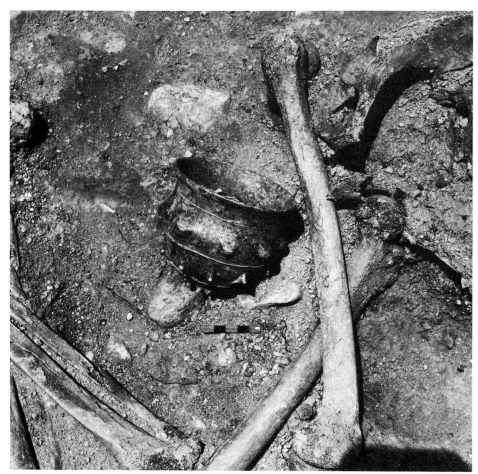

11. Excavated glass bowl with ornamental protrusions *in situ*

Each of these routes involves arduous, lengthy travel over rugged mountains by mule, making the Dailaman valley, geographically, a nearly inaccessible natural redoubt two thousand meters above sea level. It is cool (12 to 13 degrees Centigrade) in the morning and evening even in midsummer. Snow falls as early as mid-October and stays on the ground until around May, cutting off traffic to the lower region completely.

In summer, however, the valley offers spectacular scenery to compensate for the harsh winter. There is abundant grass for grazing sheep and goats, and rich fields of grain. The Sia-rud, or Black River, flows from east to west through low green hills that run north to south from the ridges of the Elburz Mountains. Clustered on the tops and slopes of these hills were found the prehistoric tombs and those of the Partho-Sassanian period. Following is a summary of finds made in this area.

1. *Hassani-mahale tomb VII.* Hassani-mahale hill,[1] two kilometers southwest of Ispeli, is one of the hills on the west side of the road from Ispeli to Dailaman. According to what local people told the Tokyo University expedition, cut-glass pieces

had been found on this hill. In the summer of 1964, during the digging of a two-meter-square trench in a relatively flat area on top of the hill, at a depth of approximately thirty centimeters a hole opened to the tip of a pick and a shaft grave was disclosed. This burial site, labeled Hassani-mahale tomb VII, fortunately had not been pillaged, nor did it show signs of crumbling. The burial goods within were recovered intact.

The entrance to tomb VII, which faces southwest, was covered by several stones. Its width is approximately 42.5 cm. and its height approximately 70 cm. The interior is ellipsoid; the major axis is 155 cm., the minor axis 107.5 cm., and the height approximately 95 cm.

The bones of a mature female, buried in a contracted position on her left side with her head to the northeast, were found in the innermost part of the tomb along the north side. The bones were poorly preserved compared to other human bones discovered on Hassani-mahale hill. One glass bowl with ornamental protrusions (fig. 11) was found; this had been placed by the woman's thighs. Befitting the grave of a woman, spinning whorls, a hand mirror, scissors, toilet articles, and ornaments were predominant among the burial goods. Numerous blue and white round glass beads that must originally have formed a necklace were found near the leg bones. Tomb VII is estimated to date from the late Parthian or early Sassanian dynasty, that is, from about the time of Christ to perhaps the third century.

2. *Hassani-mahale tomb IV*. This tomb is a typical subterranean shaft grave on the southern slope of Hassani-mahale hill and, except for some crumbling of the ceiling of the grave chamber, was in very good condition when excavated. The bones of another mature female, also buried in a contracted position on her left side, were discovered.

Burial goods were abundant and had been placed about fifty centimeters from the head. A phallus-shaped faience pendant and a flat rectangular glass pendant with a nude female figure in relief (fig. 12) were among the ornaments found. Judging from the age of the surrounding artifacts, this tomb also dates from some time between the first and third centuries.

3. *Ghalekuti tomb I-V*. The Ghalekuti hills consist of four nearly parallel ridges running north to south approximately three kilometers east-northeast of Ispeli.[2] The excavators, who included the author, designated these hills, from the west, hill IV, hill I, hill II, and hill III.

Tomb I-V, on the eastern slope of hill I, had been considerably damaged, probably unwittingly by farmers rather than by grave robbers. Bones of a mature male were found, but they had been displaced and it was not possible to establish clearly the size and shape of the burial mound. Numerous artifacts were discovered (fig. 13).

12. Glass pendant

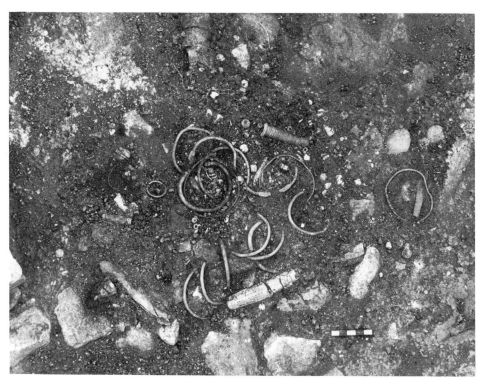

13. Excavated ornaments *in situ*

Two small glass jars (one of them core-molded) and two strings of an inlaid glass bead necklace (pls. 39, 40) were among the finds. I originally estimated that the tomb dated from before the fourth century B.C.,[3] but in a more recent paper I revised the date to the fourth or third century B.C., meaning that the tomb was of the late Achaemenid or early Parthian dynasty.

4. *Ghalekuti tomb I-IX.* Six skeletons were found at this site near the top of hill I. The bodies had been buried one on top of another but obviously not all during the same period. Two inlaid beads were found, of virtually the same type as those excavated from Ghalekuti tomb I-V, and belonging to the same period. This tomb, like most on hill I, is also a shaft grave.

5. *Ghalekuti tomb II-III.* Bones of a mature male buried in a contracted position on his side were found here. Appropriately, many weapons had been buried with him, but beads and other ornaments were also plentiful. Numerous beads, including some inlaid ones, were found near the right forearm. The age of this tomb is estimated to be the same as that of Ghalekuti tombs I-V and I-IX.

6. *Noruz-mahale tomb B-IV.* Noruz-mahale hill is approximately 1.5 kilometers east of Ispeli on the way to the Ghalekuti hills. Signs of grave plundering were apparent when the Tokyo University team visited the site in 1960, and we learned from villagers that many glass vessels had been found there earlier.[4] Tomb B-IV is a shaft grave covered by a mound. Bones

of a mature male and a mature female lying on their sides next to each other in contracted positions were found. Near the female's right elbow was a spinning whorl, and three small white glass beads were found near her chest, along with six small onyx beads.

7. *Noruz-mahale tomb D-III.* This is an oval-shaped shaft grave with a mound. A one- or two-year-old child was buried in a contracted position on its side. Along with other ornaments, blue glass beads were found near the child's legs.

8. *Noruz-mahale tomb D-IV.* This is a subterranean shaft grave. Bones of a mature female lying on her side in a contracted position were found in the northwestern part of the burial chamber. A glass spinning whorl placed on a pebble was discovered near the right shoulder. A fragment from the neck of a glass bottle set on a copper hand mirror, south of the spinning whorl, and a pair of gold earrings were also found. In addition, various glass beads were found near the chin and chest, along with onyx, agate, and amber beads. The mosaic beads are especially noteworthy.

Judging from the style of the iron weapons and the polished earthenware with a dark brown ground found in tombs in the Noruz-mahale hills, the three sites at which glass objects were discovered date from the late Parthian period, around the first to third century.

9. *Khoramrud tomb A-IV.* The Khoramrud site is some two kilometers downstream near the mountain torrent that flows along the east side of the Ghalekuti hills. One undisturbed grave and seventeen plundered graves were investigated. Each was a subterranean shaft grave, similar to those in the Noruz-mahale area. Some of the funerary objects had escaped the grave robbers, including a glass ring (fig. 70). These tombs are estimated to date from the first to third century, the same dating as that for the tombs at Noruz-mahale.[5]

SHIMAM Rudbar is located midway along the road connecting Qazvin with Resht on the Caspian Sea coast. In 1969 Mohandes Ali Hakemi of the Iranian Center of Archaeological Research uncovered a glass bowl, decorated with circular facets, in a tomb of the late Parthian dynasty at Shimam in the Rudbar area. The bowl (excavation no. 124; figs. 14, 15) has an outward-curving lip.

OTHER REGIONS Around 1960, stories of glass vessels found in Luristan and Azerbaijan were heard from time to time from antique dealers in Teheran, but as there was no evidence to corroborate these stories, it is accurate to say that most of the Persian glassware definitely attributable to the Partho-Sassanian period discovered up to now has come from tombs in Gilan.

14, 15. Glass bowl with circular facets from Shimam

29

Vessel Shapes, Production Methods, and Ornamental Techniques

Because most of the glass objects from the Partho-Sassanian period have been obtained from grave robbers, specimens discovered by scientific archaeological excavation being extremely rare, it is very difficult to distinguish between works of the Parthian dynasty and those of the Sassanian. The problem is further complicated by the fact that the glass objects found recently in tombs of the Partho-Sassanian period naturally include both works indigenous to Persia, made in the Iranian highlands, and Syrian glassware made in the eastern Mediterranean coastal region and imported to the Iranian highlands.

Here I will disregard niceties of dating and provenance and will consider together all the glass objects known or reported to have been found in the Iranian highlands, classifying them by shape and examining methods of manufacture and ornamentation. At the same time, we must acknowledge the importance of the question of the importation of Syrian glass, both for understanding the nature of Persian glass and for studying the question of East-West cultural exchange.

SHAPES   In general, glass vessels should be classified according to shape, but of course use, size, and method of manufacture must also be considered. (Many glass vessels are smaller than their earthenware or metal counterparts, due in part to the limitations of glass as a material.) Basically, glass vessels can be classified according to the following seven shapes: (I) bowl or cup, (II) footed cup, (III) beaker, (IV) rhyton, (V) dish, (VI) handled bottle, and (VII) vase. Each of these categories can be further divided into several subcategories according to variations in shape.

I. *Bowl or cup*. This kind of vessel has a wide lip, a small, flat base, and a cup-shaped body. It is divided into three subgroups according to the shape of the rim:

I-A. The rim is either vertical or curved slightly inward (pls. 1–5).

I-B. The rim is turned slightly outward (pls. 6–8).

I-C. The rim curves outward; there is a clearly defined neck. Some vessels of subgroups I-A and I-B have a foot or its equivalent (pls. 11–14, 16).

II. *Footed cup*. A foot is attached to a bowl-shaped or elongated cup (pls. 17 left, 18–20).

III. *Beaker*. This classification refers to a conical vessel with a pointed bottom, either a straight or a curved body, and a wide rim. There are two subgroups:

III–A. The rim is vertical (pl. 21).

III–B. The rim is turned outward (pls. 22, 23).

IV. *Rhyton*. This vessel has a spout at either top or bottom (pl. 24).

V. *Dish*. This classification refers to a relatively shallow, round-bottomed vessel with walls that either are vertical or curve outward (pls. 25–27).

VI. *Handled bottle*. This refers to a bulging, pitcher-shaped vessel with a constricted neck and a projecting lip (pls. 28, 29).

VII. *Vase*. The rounded body and the neck of this type of vessel are clearly distinguishable, and the diameter of the rim is smaller than that of the body (pls. 30, 34, 35).

In addition to the above, there is an exceptional form, the boat-shaped cup. This shape was probably copied from metalware.

16. Glass vase with handles bearing the name of Sargon II

PRODUCTION METHODS   Two techniques, mold-blowing and free-blowing, were used in Persia to make glass vessels during the Partho-Sassanian period, and two kinds of vessels were produced: those with thick walls and those with thin. The thick-walled vessels were made chiefly by mold-blowing, while the thin-walled ones were made by free-blowing.

At an earlier period, however, it was the grind-and-polish method that was used in the Iranian highlands, probably introduced from Mesopotamia during the Achaemenid dynasty. Several pieces of glassware have been found at Nimrud, the capital of the Assyrian empire in northern Mesopotamia. Of these, a green glass vase with handles, bearing the name of King Sargon II (721–704 B.C.), is especially well known (fig. 16; this vase is now in the British Museum). This work was made by grinding out a block of glass, then finishing both the inside and the outside surfaces by polishing.

Fragments of a rock-crystal bowl were also discovered in the ruins of the palace at Nimrud. The shape of this bowl is very similar to that of the glass vessels also found there, and it is believed that the glass vessels were made by copying the techniques used for rock crystal and other stoneware. Although there is as yet no concrete evidence, it can reasonably be concluded that the grind-and-polish method of making glassware was well established in northern Mesopotamia by the eighth century B.C. and that it spread to the Iranian highlands with the rise of the Achaemenid dynasty in Persia. After the fall of this dynasty, the production of glass in Mesopotamia also declined but seems to have revived in the later Parthian dynasty.

I myself believe that the grind-and-polish method evolved into the mold-blowing method by which thick glass vessels were made in the Iranian highlands. Dr. Axel von Saldern has criticized this theory, suggesting that the manufacturing technique did not involve a mold but was rather the free-

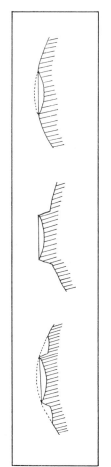

17. Various types of facets

blowing method.[6] However, a report of the Shōsō-in Office published more recently states, concerning the glass bowl in the Shōsō-in, that "numerous small scratches were seen when this vessel was viewed against a black paper background. This indicates that the vessel was not free-blown but was made using a mold. Apparently these scratches occurred because the inner surface of the mold was coarse."[7] I continue to hold to the theory of the mold-blowing method and believe that the free-blowing method was probably introduced from Syria around the time of Christ.

ORNAMENTAL TECHNIQUES   The latter half of the Parthian dynasty extended from the first century A.D. until it gave way to the Sassanian dynasty in 226. Along with metalworking, glass manufacture flourished during this period, and there was an increasing demand for Persian goods in both the Occident and the Orient. The demand for thick glass vessels was particularly great, with some being transported via the Silk Road as far east as Japan.

The types of ornamentation on glass vessels in the Parthian and Sassanian dynasties are classified as follows: (I) facets, (II) ornamentation with trailed glass strings, (III) ornamental protrusions, (IV) ornamental blobs, (V) pattern-mold decoration, and (VI) feathered ornamentation. Of these the first, especially circular facets cut into thick glass, is the most common. Following is a brief discussion of the techniques used in each of the above categories.

I. *Facets.* Grindstones clearly were used to cut decorations into the surface of thick glass vessels. There are various kinds of cut decorations, including engraved lines, circular facets, tortoise-shell-pattern facets, and oval facets, though circular facets are the most common.

I-1. Ornamentation with engraved lines, both straight and curved. The technique employed is exactly the same as that for engraving pottery and must have developed from the methods used to decorate pottery.

I-2. Ornamentation with circular facets. There are three kinds of circular facets (fig. 17):

(A) Concave facets (fig. 17 top). The vessel is decorated by cutting into the glass body, a common style we might call the "Shōsō-in type." Among the bowls found in Gilan Province, this ornamental style is the most common.

(B) Facets in relief (figs. 17 middle, 36; pl. 11). A blank bowl with raised circular facets is made in a mold, then the top surface of each facet is cut like a concave lens. Fragments of a glass bowl found on Okinoshima provide an example of this style. This "Okinoshima type" of cut decoration was not as popular in the Partho-Sassanian period as the Shōsō-in type, and only a few specimens with this kind of ornamentation have been found in Gilan. Since contemporary stoneware, such as agate and rock-crystal seals and earrings, was decorated by this method, it is reasonable to conclude that a technique first developed to decorate stoneware was adapted for ornamenting glass vessels.

(C) Double facets (fig. 17 bottom; pls. 12, 13). At first glance, this appears to combine the Shōsō-in and Okinoshima types of decoration. The surface of the inner circular facet of the double facet is flush with the surface of the vessel. This indicates that the inner circular facet was cut into the body of the vessel itself, exactly as in the Shōsō-in type of ornamentation. Then the outer circle was hollowed, leaving some chamfer around the inner facet. Thus the finished ornamentation gives the effect of the Okinoshima type, but from the standpoint of technique it is a variation of the Shōsō-in type. Because fragments of a glass bowl with this kind of cut decoration have been excavated from the Kamigamo district in Kyoto, the style may be termed the "Kamigamo type."

I-3. Tortoise-shell-pattern facets (pl. 4). This design features contiguous circular facets covering the entire surface. This type of decoration is found not only on glass vessels but also on embossed metal vessels contemporary with the bowl illustrated.

I-4. Oval facets (pl. 6). Oval facets are usually cut with some space between them, unlike circular facets, which are cut closely adjoining each other.

II. *Ornamentation with trailed glass strings*. This technique is executed by winding thinly stretched glass strings of the same color as the vessel itself around the rim section. The origin of the technique can be traced to Syrian glassware.

III. *Ornamental protrusions*. Large (pl. 10) or small (pls. 14, 15) protrusions resembling warts are arranged either regularly or irregularly on the vessel. In some instances, small protrusions ringing the base of a bowl form feet. Apparently the protrusions were made by scratching the surface of the glass or, for large protrusions, pinching it with a tool before the blown glass had set. This technique was ingeniously devised to take advantage of the nature of glass. As with the glass-string technique, apparently it did not originate in Persia, for it is seen in Syrian glass along with the glass-string method. To go still further back in history, it is said that the ornamental protrusions on Minoan pottery in the so-called Barbotine style of the early Bronze Age (c. 1800 B.C.) were inspired by the protrusions on crab shells. It would not be at all strange, then, if glass craftsmen in the Syrian region were also inspired by the forms of shells to develop this type of ornamentation.

Object \ Row no.	Base	One	Two	Three	Four	Five	Six	Seven	Plates and Figures
Gilan find 1	1	7	13	13					Pl. 2
Gilan find 2	1	7	14	15	14				Pl. 3
Gilan find 3	1	7	19	19	19	19			Pl. 1, Fig. 20
Gilan find 4	1	7	23	23	23	23	23	23	Pl. 4, Fig. 21
Shōsō-in bowl	1	7	18	18	18	18			Figs. 28, 29
Ankan bowl	1	7	18	18	18	18			Fig. 30

Table 1. Number of facets in each row of selected glass bowls

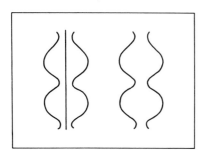

18. Pattern-mold decoration

19. Glass tube beads

IV. *Ornamental blobs.* Blobs of dark blue glass were used to decorate the surfaces of amber-colored or pale green glass vessels. Many of the vessels embellished in this way were cone-shaped rhytons. This technique was extensively used to decorate Syrian and Roman glass objects, and was popular around the fourth and early fifth centuries. Vessels thus ornamented are among the artifacts found in the Iranian highlands, but many appear to have been taken there from the Syrian region.

V. *Pattern-mold decoration.* During the Partho-Sassanian period, ornamental reliefs were created by the use of molds. Figure 18 shows a characteristic motif made by this method, a serpentine on both sides of a center line (in some instances there is no center line). This design was extensively used on glass vessels during the first to third century (pl. 35) and also in decorating tube beads (fig. 19).

VI. *Feathered ornamentation.* This technique, used to decorate core-molded glass, can be traced back to ancient Egypt. First, a glass vessel is made by core-molding. Before the glass has set, several glass strings of different colors are wound around the body. Finally, the feathered design is achieved by combing the glass threads up and down with a rod having a hooked end. This type of ornamentation is seen on objects of the fourth to third century B.C. found in Iran, but further study is required before we can determine whether they were actually made there.

Examples of Glass Vessels

BOWLS WITH CIRCULAR FACETS (TYPE I-A)   As type I-A glass bowls, ornamented with concave circular facets (pls. 1–5),

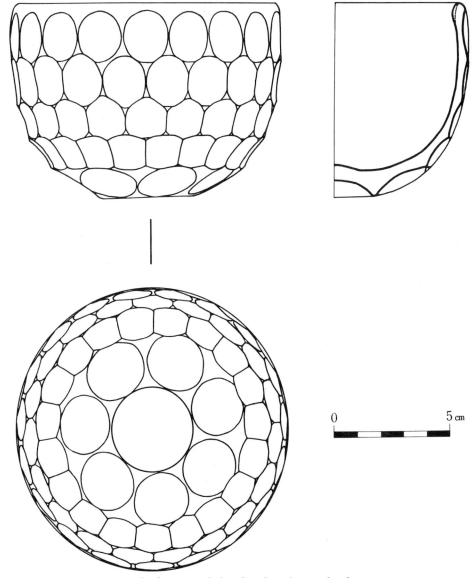

20. Scale drawing of glass bowl with circular facets

are the most plentiful among the finds from Gilan, this type of decoration was presumably the most popular in Persia during the Partho-Sassanian period.

Probably because they were buried for well over a thousand years, both the inside and the outside surfaces of these vessels have effloresced considerably. For the most part, the colors have changed to gold or silver, but the original light brown or pale green glass remains partly visible.

The rim of this type of bowl generally is either vertical or slightly turned in, and the interior of the base is usually slightly convex. The exterior surface is decorated with many circular facets in horizontal rows, with a large circular facet at the base (fig. 20). One characteristic common to vessels of this type is that seven smaller facets surround the large central facet at the base; in a variant design, there are seven large and seven small circular facets around the base instead of seven similar-sized facets (pl. 4, fig. 21).

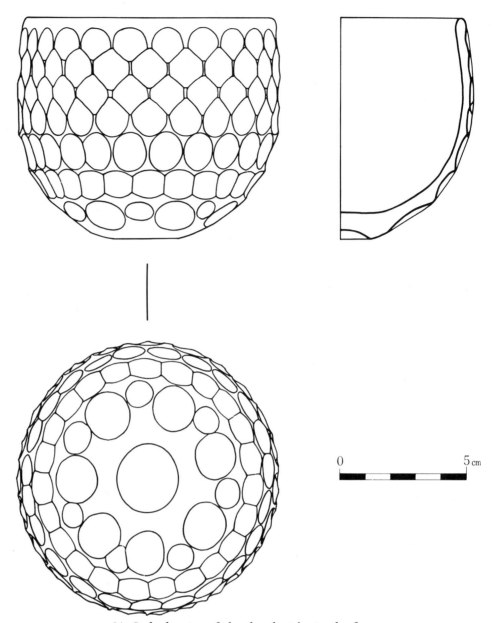

21. Scale drawing of glass bowl with circular facets

These bowls can be divided roughly into three size categories: large (diameter at the lip more than 11 cm.), medium (diameter at the lip 10 to 11 cm.), and small (diameter at the lip less than 10 cm.).

At present there is no conclusive evidence indicating when and where this kind of glass bowl was made. Chemical analysis shows that the glass contains the same elements as ordinary soda glass, with no lead content.[8] This would also indicate that the bowls are made of the same kind of glass as Syrian ware. However, it is thought that this kind of glass bowl was made near the Caspian Sea because more than one hundred bowls of this type have been found in Gilan Province; the shape and manufacturing technique are typical of the ancient Middle East, the excavation sites face the Caspian Sea north of the Elburz Mountains, and the geographic and climatic conditions of this region are similar to those of the eastern Mediterranean coastal region, where Syrian glass was made.

The bowls found in Gilan are thought to have been made as early as the first century A.D. This belief is based on the facts that an identical type of bowl, found at Sudagilan in the Azerbaijan region of the Soviet Union, is thought to have been made sometime during the first to third century because Parthian and Roman coins of that time were also found at the site, and that the mound-tomb excavations in the Ufimusco highlands in the central Urals, a site yielding the same kind of glass bowl, are estimated to date to the third or fourth century. The popularity of thick glass bowls with circular facets was at its height in Persia during the Sassanian dynasty, but such bowls were no longer being manufactured by the beginning of the Islamic period around the latter half of the seventh century.

Even a brief look at the distribution of sites where bowls of this type have been found indicates the range of East-West cultural exchange.

1. Mesopotamian Region

Ctesiphon: This city on the Tigris in central Iraq was the capital of the Parthian and Sassanian dynasties. Ten fragments of glass bowls with circular facets (fig. 22), thought to be from seven different bowls, have been found here.

Kish: One fragment of a glass bowl with circular facets (fig. 23) has been found at this site east of Babylon. Judging from the age of the ruins in which it was uncovered, the finders estimated that the bowl is from the sixth century A.D.

Ain Sinu: This is a site dating to the Roman period in northern Mesopotamia. One fragment of a glass bowl similar to a type I-A bowl but with a slightly wider rim has been found here.

2. Syrian Region

Palmyra: No glass bowls have been found at Palmyra, a caravan city on the Silk Road that prospered for several centuries following the time of Christ. However, a tomb carving found here of an object thought to be a glass bowl suggests that the Palmyrans used this kind of vessel.

3. Eastern Mediterranean Region

Petra: One fragment of a glass bowl with circular facets (fig. 24), dated to the first to second century A.D., has been discovered at Petra in southern Jordan.

The regions cited above are all west of the Iranian highlands. Regions to the north and west are discussed below.

4. Azerbaijan Region

Sudagilan: One glass bowl with circular facets (fig. 25) has been found, along with Parthian and Roman coins, at this site on the left bank of the Kura River in the Azerbaijan region of the Soviet Union. An excavation report dates the tomb in which the bowl was found to the first to third century A.D.

22. Fragment of glass bowl with circular facets from Ctesiphon

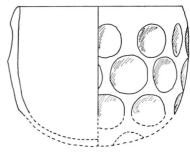

23. Fragment of glass bowl with circular facets from Kish

24. Glass bowl with circular facets from Petra

25. Glass bowl with circular facets from Sudagilan

26. Glass bowl with circular facets from Kurgan

27. Glass bowl painted on silk banner from Tunhuang

5. *Armenian Region*

Kurgan: A type I-A glass bowl (fig. 26) has been excavated at this site in Garni in the Armenian Republic, part of the Soviet Union.

6. *Central Ural Region*

Karl Marx site: A type I-A bowl has been excavated at this site of an ancient community in the town of Karl Marx in the Ufimusco highlands in the central Urals. The mound tomb in which the bowl was found is estimated to date to the third or fourth century A.D.

7. *Central Asia*

Kum Tura: Early in this century, Dr. Albert von le Coq found a fragment of a glass bowl with circular facets in the vicinity of Kum Tura during his exploration of Central Asia.

Tunhuang: A painted silk banner dating to around the eighth century A.D. was found at this site in Kansu Province, northwestern China, and is now in the British Museum. A green bowl with circular facets, held in the raised right hand of the Bodhisattva Avalokitesvara, is depicted on the banner (fig. 27).[9] The bowl appears to be of transparent glass, for the fingers show through. This painted glass bowl differs from those excavated only in that the lip of the bowl is trimmed with metal. The painting is positive evidence that glass bowls had already been taken to this area.

8. *China and the Korean Peninsula*

Since the 1950s the land-development movement in China has been accompanied by vigorous archaeological activity, and glass objects, many of them thin-walled, blown vessels, are among the many artifacts discovered. Before World War II, glass vessels were also excavated in the Korean Peninsula from mound tombs of the ancient kingdom of Silla in southern Korea (57 B.C.–A.D. 935). The sites include the Kum Kwan Chong, Kum Yung Chong, and Suh Bong Chong tumuli. All the glass objects found in the Korean Peninsula are thin-walled vessel of the Syrian type. Not a single fragment of glass with circular facets, of the type being discussed in this section, has been discovered either in China proper or in the Korean Peninsula. But it is clear that glass bowls were taken to China by caravan across Central Asia, as indicated by the following passage from the poem *Glass Bowls* by Pong Nei, written during the Chin dynasty (265–420): "across the perilous sands and over the rugged Pamirs . . ."

9. *Japan*

Shōsō-in: The magnificent glass bowl with circular facets (figs. 28, 29) in this eighth-century repository connected to the Tōdai-ji temple in Nara is believed to have been donated to the temple by Emperor Shōmu in 752 at the time of the ceremony dedicating the newly constructed Daibutsu, a huge bronze image of the Buddha, at the temple. However, there is

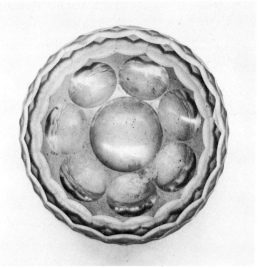

28, 29. Glass bowl with circular facets in the Shōsō-in

no documentation for this. The bowl is exactly like those excavated in Gilan. It is beautifully finished, and, probably because of the care with which it has been stored, it shows no sign of efflorescence. The bowl has a slightly constricted rim and is made of light brown glass, which spectroscopic analysis shows to be soda glass.[10]

Tumulus of Emperor Ankan: The glass bowl (fig. 30) from the tumulus of Emperor Ankan (r. 531–35) in Osaka Prefecture, said to have been found there during the Edo period (1603–1868), is almost identical to the Shōsō-in bowl. The Ankan bowl is also light brown in color, and it is about the same size as the one in the Shōsō-in. Because the two bowls are so similar, the question arises whether they were made at the same time and in the same region. The Japanese themselves could not possibly have had the skills to do this kind of work at the time of Emperor Ankan, or even in the eighth century. Furthermore, no indication that this type of work was done in China or Korea has been found to date. It is virtually certain, therefore, that these bowls were made, along with numerous others, in Gilan and taken to Japan via Central Asia. Judging from the stratum where it was found, the bowl from Emperor Ankan's tomb was buried no later than the second half of the sixth century. Assuming that the two bowls were taken to Japan at the same time, the one in the Shōsō-in was somehow preserved in Japan until the mid-eighth century, when it was donated to the Tōdai-ji. It is impossible to pinpoint the precise age of these two bowls until the age of similar bowls found in Gilan has been determined. It seems clear, however, that at least the one from the tomb of Emperor Ankan dates from the Sassanian dynasty before the sixth century. The bowl in the Shōsō-in can be presumed to belong to approximately the same period.[11]

30. Glass bowl with circular facets (Tokyo National Museum)

39

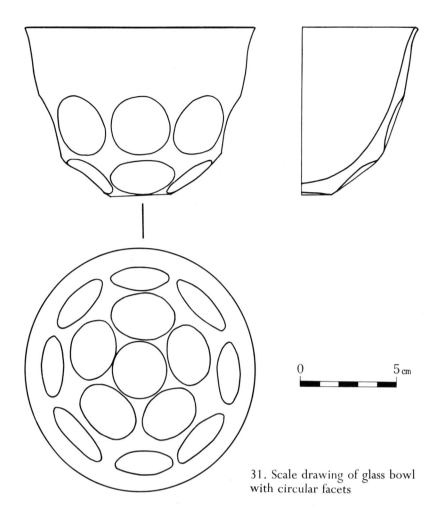

31. Scale drawing of glass bowl
with circular facets

Bowls with Circular Facets (Type I-B) The type I-B glass bowl (pls. 6–8, fig. 31) is a vessel of thick glass through the body to the base, like the type I-A bowl. It is characterized by an outward-curving rim, unlike type I-A, and also by the absence of a convex interior bulge at the base. The glass is usually pale green and contains many air bubbles. The surface of the vessel has concave circular facets, like the I-A type, but the facets are much larger than those on type I-A works. In addition to the large facet at the base, there are two rows of circular or oval facets. Usually the lower row has five or six facets and the top row eight to twelve. Some of the more intricately ornamented I-B bowls have vertical or horizontal incised lines in the spaces between the facets (fig. 32).

Object \ Row no.	Base	Lower	Upper	Plates and Figures
Gilan find 1	1	5	8	Pl. 7, Fig. 31
Gilan find 2	1	5	10	Pl. 6
Shimam find	1	6	12	Fig. 14

Table 2. Number of facets in each row of selected glass bowls

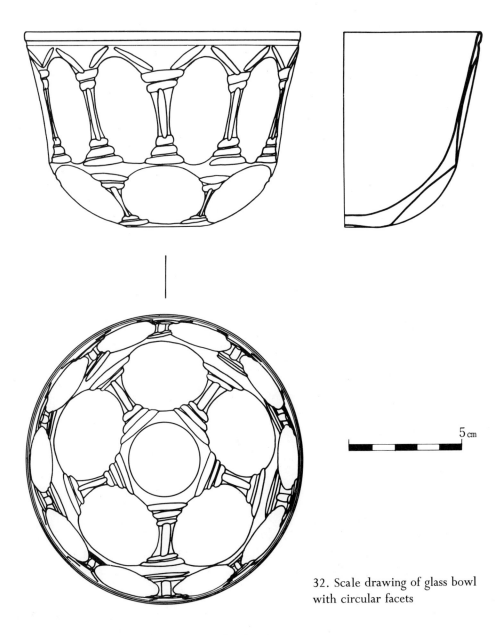

32. Scale drawing of glass bowl with circular facets

A glass bowl of this type was discovered in 1969 at Shimam in the Rudbar region. Figures 14 and 15 show this vessel, which is of pale green glass although most of the surface has effloresced. The rim is turned slightly outward, and the glass thickens toward the base. The height of the vessel is 8 cm., and the diameter at the lip is 11.8 cm. There is a circular facet (diameter 2.5 cm.) at the base, with six facets (diameter 2.7 cm.) surrounding it. There are twelve oval facets (4 × 2.3 cm.) in the upper row. In addition, there are two ornamental incised horizontal lines between the facets in the upper and lower rows and four ornamental incised horizontal lines on the rim section.

Because of this find, it is assumed that type I-A and type I-B glass bowls were made at the same time during the late Parthian dynasty. However, far fewer type I-B bowls are known, and probably manufacture of this type of bowl was not very widespread. Presumably the bowls were produced in the Iranian highlands, for this style is not seen in Syrian glassware.

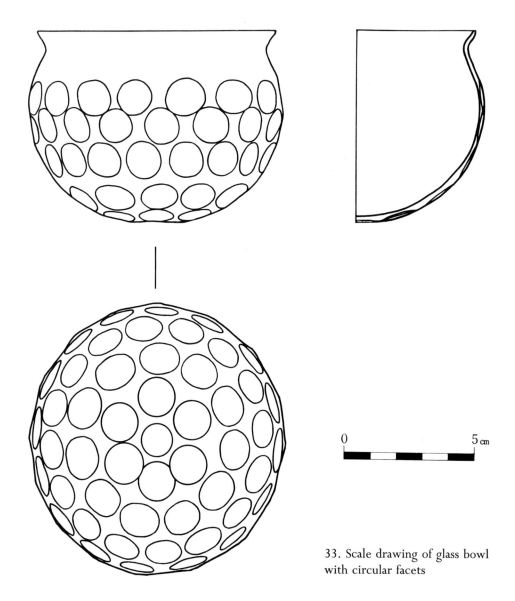

33. Scale drawing of glass bowl
with circular facets

34. Glass bowl with circular facets
from Seleucia

35. Glass bowl with circular facets
(Tokyo National Museum)

BOWLS WITH CIRCULAR FACETS (TYPE I-C) Type I-C is characterized by a distinctly constricted neck and a lip that curves
outward (pl. 9, fig. 33). Usually this type of vessel is made of
very thin white glass shaped by blowing. The entire surface
of the bowl is decorated with circular facets, just as are type
I-A bowls. The piece shown in figure 33 is said to have been
found in Kharsa Khaneh in the Dailaman region. It has a circular facet at the base and rows of six, eleven, sixteen, and
sixteen circular facets on the body of the bowl, exactly like
I-A bowls. Although the walls of the vessel are thin, each
facet is concave. The bowl was made in either the late Parthian or the early Sassanian dynasty, judging from the date of
the ruins in which it was discovered.

Perhaps because this type of bowl is easily broken, it is
rarely found today. The Iraq National Museum in Baghdad
owns one (fig. 34), said to have been found in Seleucia. There
have been no reports of this kind of vessel from Central Asia,
China, or Korea. In Japan, a cobalt blue glass dish with a white
glass bowl placed on it (fig. 35) were unearthed in 1963 from
tomb 126 during the archaeological excavation of the Niizawa

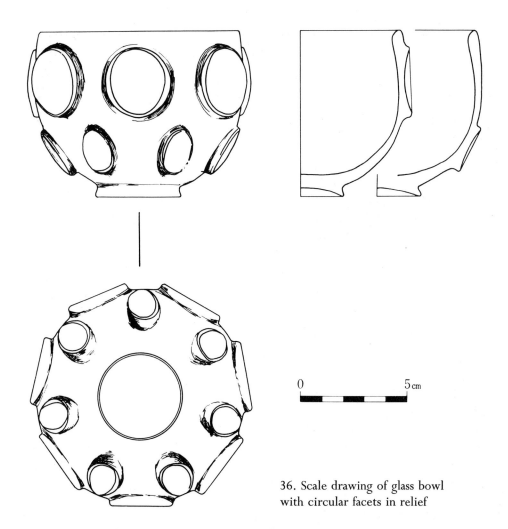

36. Scale drawing of glass bowl
with circular facets in relief

Senzuka tombs in Nara Prefecture.[12] The bowl is made of thin glass, with circular facets similar to those of type I-C bowls, and is characterized by combined use of concave circular facets and circular facets made by rubbing.

There is absolutely no reason to believe that this bowl, presumed to date to the fourth or fifth century, was made in Japan. It is reasonable to suppose that it was imported from the Iranian highlands.

Bowls with Facets in Relief Glass bowls with facets in relief (pl. 11, fig. 36) were found in Gilan, as were type I-A glass bowls with concave circular facets, but much less often. The bowl shown in figure 36 has a slightly constricted rim and a foot. There are seven circular facets in relief in the upper row and the same number of fingertip-size oval facets in relief in the lower row. The blank bowl with its relief pattern was made in a mold, and the surface of each circular (or sometimes somewhat oval) facet was then hollowed to concavity. All bowls embellished with relief facets were made in molds. Usually the raised circular facet at the base (fig. 37), which functions as a foot, is somewhat larger than the circular facets in the upper row. Vessels of this type are made of light brown or pale green translucent glass containing many air bubbles.

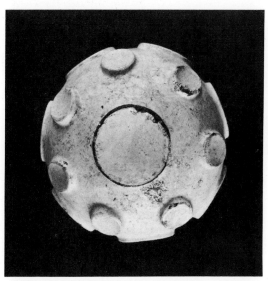

37. Glass bowl with circular facets in relief

38. Stone seals

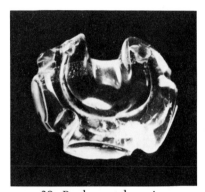

39. Rock-crystal earring

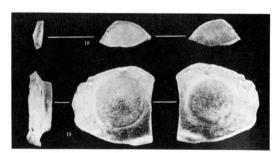

40. Fragments of glass bowl found on Okino-shima (Munakata Shrine)

Ornamentation with facets in relief was very popular, and was also utilized for decorating Persian stone seals (fig. 38) and rock-crystal earrings (fig. 39). It is impossible to conclude on the basis of present evidence which of the two styles of ornamentation, concave circular facets or facets in relief, appeared first. But for technical considerations it is reasonable to assume that the relief-facet style is older because, as mentioned earlier, glass-cutting techniques evolved from those used for cutting vessels of stone, such as rock crystal, and we can be fairly confident that a decorative style, such as that of facets cut in relief, used originally for stoneware was applied very early to glass.

It may well have been aesthetic reasons that impelled the evolution of decorative techniques uniquely suited to glass. The sparkle of glass when held to the light affords a spectacle that can be produced by no other material. To take the bowl in the Shōsō-in as an example: the exterior is beautiful, but since the bowl was used as a drinking vessel, it was probably carved in such a way as to be most impressive when seen with the light coming through it. The full potential of glass as an aesthetic medium cannot be realized when techniques used for decorating stone or pottery are used to ornament glass. Craftsmen must gradually have come to realize that glass could be better exploited by cutting facets into the body of the vessel itself than by molding facets in relief. Thus I believe that what originally were probably effects achieved by chance during the process of cutting facets in relief were admired, and that these chance effects led to the development of the technique of cutting concave circular facets, creating a style particularly suited to glass.

The earlier technique did not, however, simply disappear. Having emerged in the late Parthian dynasty, it was still in vogue, along with the later, concave-facet technique, during the Sassanian dynasty and continued to be fashionable into the early Islamic period.

Two very important fragments of a glass bowl ornamented with facets in relief (fig. 40) have been found on Okinoshima, an isolated Japanese island in the Genkai Sea east of northern Kyushu. Historically, this island's location made it important as a center of sea traffic between the Korean Peninsula and northern Kyushu. The fragments, discovered in the ruins of a religious site of the late Tumulus period (approximately sixth to seventh century), are of a glass bowl very like the bowls with facets in relief found in Gilan.

The two fragments found on Okinoshima are undoubtedly part of the same vessel. They are of pale green glass containing many air bubbles, and on one there is an entire circular facet in relief. According to one report,[13] the fragments apparently come from a glass bowl that had nine circular facets

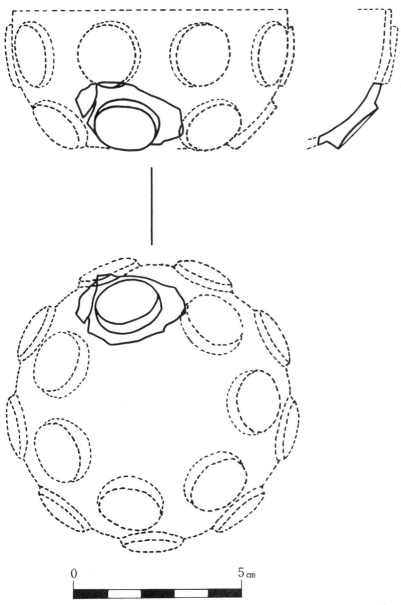

41. Scale drawing of reconstructed glass fragments found on Okinoshima

in relief in the upper row and seven in the lower row. The complete facet that remains is believed to belong to the lower row. (Bowls from Gilan have seven circular facets in relief in each row, and a large facet functioning as a foot at the base.) In any case, the facet on the Okinoshima fragment was made by molding, as were the relief facets on vessels found in Gilan, not by the technique of application.

There is no doubt that this bowl was taken to Japan from the Iranian highlands via Central Asia prior to the sixth or seventh century, just as were the bowls with concave circular facets, and was not made in Japan or the Korean Peninsula. The Okinoshima fragments suggest the importance of this island in early East-West contacts. These bits of glass, the bowl from the tumulus of Emperor Ankan, and the Shōsō-in bowl indicate one aspect of the Japanese national character in the prehistoric period: a receptive attitude to the importation of culture.[14]

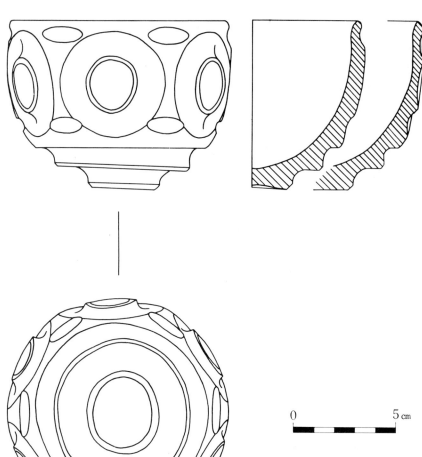

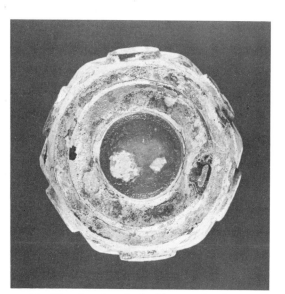

43. Glass bowl with double circular facets

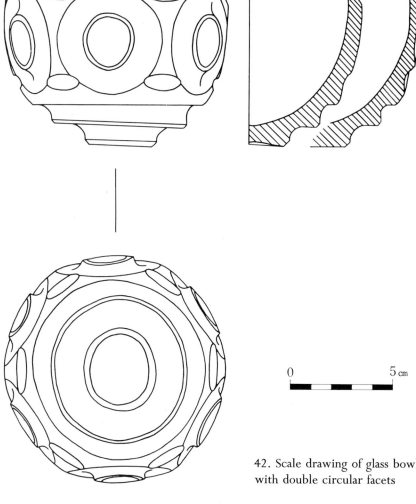

42. Scale drawing of glass bowl with double circular facets

44. Glass bowl with double circular facets

BOWLS WITH DOUBLE CIRCULAR FACETS The bowls shown in plates 12 and 13 and figures 42–44 are type I-A with a slightly constricted rim. This type of vessel is the rarest of those found in the Iranian highlands. It is bowl-shaped but has a double-tiered foot and is the thickest kind of glass bowl.

There is a total of six double circular facets on the example illustrated in plate 12 and figure 42. The facets are evenly spaced, an average of .35 cm. apart. The diameter of the outer circle is approximately 5 cm., that of the inner circle 2.7 cm. At first glance the inner circle appears to have been made by carving a circular facet in relief following molding, as was done on the fragment found on Okinoshima. The diameter of the surface of the relief facet is smaller, though only slightly, than that of the part of the relief adjoining the body of the vessel, and the facet is planed concave, leaving a thick chamfer of the original surface around it. The triangular space created above and below the row of double circular facets is embellished with engraved horizontal lines. Some works of this type are decorated with concave circular facets in addition to engraved horizontal lines.

Usually the foot is in doubled-tiered form, as seen in figure

43. The upper tier of the foot, adjoining the body of this bowl, is larger than the lower tier. A shallow round facet is cut over the entire surface of the foot except for the chamfer left along its circumference. It is believed that the chamfer around the top and bottom tiers of the foot was not intentionally made but is what remained of the exterior surface of the bowl after the foot was carved. Therefore, presumably each tier of the foot was carved out of the body of the vessel. The inside of the bowl is a smooth curve all the way to the bottom, with no bulges. This vessel was made of translucent pale green glass containing many air bubbles, but the entire surface has effloresced to a milky white color.

45. Glass bowl with double circular facets (University of Pennsylvania Museum)

The bowl shown in plate 13 and figure 44 is said to have been found in Gilan Province. This is a thick vessel of exactly the same shape as the one shown in figure 43. However, it differs in having for decoration two rows of six double facets each. The foot of the vessel is not double-tiered. The six double circular facets in the upper row are evenly spaced, with those in the lower row skillfully placed below the spaces between the facets in the upper row. In addition, there are small circular facets between the double circular facets in the top row and a horizontal linear design engraved below the small facets.

As previously discussed, double-circular-facet decoration was achieved by cutting facets into the bowl itself, then planing the outer facets, leaving some chamfer around the inner facets. This style apparently was not popular in the Iranian highlands, as so few examples have been found. However, fragments of a glass bowl of this kind (fig. 45) were found, together with a type I-A glass bowl with concave circular facets, in the Kish ruins in the region of southern Mesopotamia bordering the western Iranian highlands. According to the excavation report,[15] the date of manufacture is estimated to be the sixth century. There is no way to prove this because no example of work with double circular facets has been found anywhere else in the Middle East. But because the ornamentation on this type of vessel is more intricate and decorative than that on vessels of the Shōsō-in type, the date of manufacture can be assigned to the late Sassanian dynasty, around the sixth century, as with the fragments excavated at Kish.

In Japan, a fragment from a similar glass bowl was found in 1964 in the Kamigamo district of Kyoto (figs. 46, 47). The fragment is nearly rectangular (6 × 4.2 cm., and 1 cm. thick). About half a double circular facet remains, and there is the edge of another double facet about .3 cm. to its right. A horizontal cut design about 1 cm. wide connects the two facets. Figure 48 is a reconstruction of the vessel based upon this fragment. The original is presumed to have been a bowl with a double-tiered foot and decorated with a row of double circular facets, similar to the bowl shown in plate 12 and figures 42 and 43.

46. Fragment of glass bowl with double circular facets (collection of Zempei Bando)

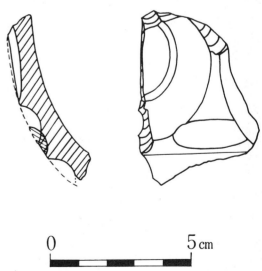

0   5 cm

47. Scale drawing of the fragment in figure 46

47

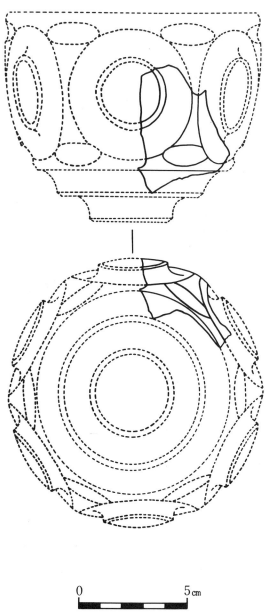

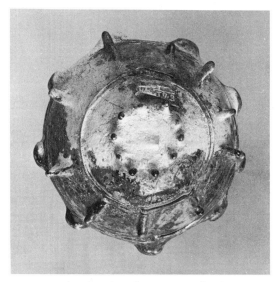

48. Scale drawing of the glass bowl excavated in Kamigamo, Kyoto

49, 50. Glass bowl with ornamental protrusions from Hassani-mahale

All glass bowls of this type would have been imported to Japan, presumably from the Iranian highlands by way of Central Asia. Since the date assigned to works of this kind found in the Middle East is around the sixth century, I will assign the same date and the same manufacturing site to the fragment discovered in Kyoto, an important find substantiating the eastward spread of Persian culture.

BOWLS WITH ORNAMENTAL PROTRUSIONS   All glass bowls of this type have either large or small ornamental protrusions resembling warts and were made of thin, pale green glass by the free-blowing method. Many such bowls have been found.

A bowl with ornamental protrusions, found in Hassani-mahale tomb VII, is shown in figures 49–51. This bowl has a

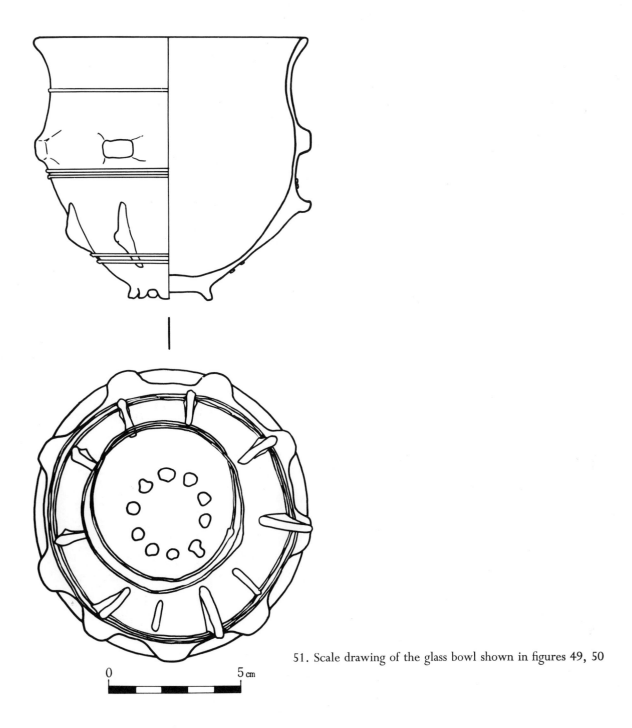

51. Scale drawing of the glass bowl shown in figures 49, 50

0   5 cm

wide rim that is turned outward. It narrows from the lip to the
neck, flares out to the middle of the body, then gradually tapers
to the base, which is almost horizontal. There are nine large
rectangular ornamental protrusions ringing the middle of the
body, with ten long keel-shaped protrusions below them. Ten
small protrusions at the base form feet. The vessel is further decorated with strings of glass of the same color as the bowl,
wound around the neck, middle, and lower part of the body.
Some vessels of this type, with the rim turned outward (pl. 15),
have a ring at the base instead of feet formed by small protrusions (pl. 10). In addition, a few footed bowl-shaped vessels
having a form typical of pottery, with a slightly constricted
rim (pl. 14), have been found.

As mentioned earlier, ornamental protrusions are believed

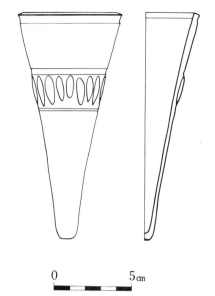

52. Scale drawing of conical beaker

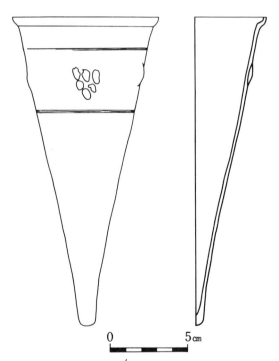

53. Scale drawing of conical beaker

to have been inspired by the protrusions on certain marine shells and the manufacturing technique to have originated in Syria. For several centuries beginning around the time of Christ this method was widely used to decorate Syrian and Roman glass. It would not be surprising if the technique was carried to the Iranian highlands during that time. Based on the age of various objects found with it, the bowl from Hassani-mahale tomb VII can be assigned to the first to third century, when this style was most popular in the Syrian region. It can be assumed that the manufacture of glass bowls with ornamental protrusions also flourished in the Iranian highlands during the same period.

VESSELS EMBELLISHED WITH BLOBS Numerous glass vessels with ornamental blobs have been found in Gilan. The conical beaker (pls. 21, 22; figs. 52, 53) is the typical form of such vessels. The design was achieved by attaching separately melted drops of dark blue glass to a white or pale green body. Many vessels so embellished were produced in about the fourth to fifth century in the Syrian region, in Alexandria, and in the Cologne region of Germany.

The conical beaker reported to have been found in Gilan (pl. 21) has incised lines as ornamentation along the rim and above and below the ornamental blobs near the middle of the body. This beaker is believed to have been used as a lamp. Vessels of the same type have been found in large numbers at the Karanis site in North Africa[16] and also in the Cologne region, and it is difficult to distinguish them from those reportedly found in Gilan. It cannot be determined, therefore, whether the latter were made in the Iranian highlands or imported.

A type I-B bowl ornamented with blobs is shown in plate 8 and figure 54. The vessel is made of transparent glass, with the rim turned outward. The top half of the bowl is decorated with a .5-cm.-wide incised line below the lip, fifteen circular cut facets, and nineteen dark blue ornamental blobs with vertical lines incised between them.

As is clear from figure 54, six circular patterns are carved on the lower half of the vessel. There are three design motifs, each motif used within two circles. It is interesting to note that one of the motifs is the widespread, ancient symbol of the swastika. The spaces between the circles are incised with vertical lines connecting two circular cuts to make a dumbbell-shaped design. The lowest part of the body is decorated with an incised line .3 cm. wide. There are five oval facets at the base. This bowl is a rare specimen. No vessel embellished with both circular cut facets and ornamental blobs has been found in either North Africa or Germany.

Taking into consideration the fact that the swastika motif is not seen on any of the finds from Karanis or the Cologne re-

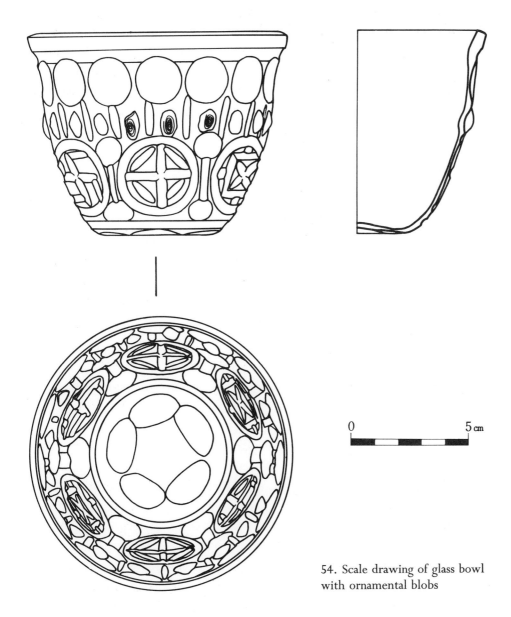

54. Scale drawing of glass bowl with ornamental blobs

gion, I would like to think that this particular vessel was made in the Iranian highlands. Of course, glass vessels with ornamental blobs not only were made in the Cologne region and in North Africa, including Alexandria and Karanis, but also must have been made on the eastern Mediterranean coast and in the Caucasus, so it is reasonable to suppose that similar vessels were made in the Iranian highlands.

The technique of ornamentation with blobs spread eastward and was used, for example, on a glass vessel found in the Kum Yung Chong tumulus in the Korean Peninsula. According to one report, this specimen is bowl-shaped, with an outward-turned rim, and is made of nearly colorless glass. Its diameter is 11 cm. at the lip, and its height is 7.6 cm. The body is decorated with two rows of small cobalt blue and purple beads melted and fused to the glass. Whether it was made in the Korean Peninsula in about the fifth century or imported from the west is uncertain, but in either case the technique by which it was manufactured originated to the west.

55 (left). Scale drawing of handled vessel

56 (right). Glass carafe (Teheran Archaeological Museum)

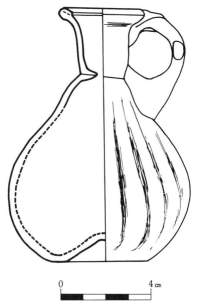

57. Carved pitcher held by the goddess Anahita,
Taq-i-Bustan

58. Glass carafe in the Shōsō-in

VESSELS WITH HANDLES Handled vessels made during the Parthian dynasty are generally small. The work shown in plate 28 and figure 55 is of green glass with many air bubbles. The round rim section is rolled, the body is pumpkin-shaped, and the handle is quite short. The distinct seam between neck and body is one of the characteristics of this period. The vessel was free-blown, and the seam is the result of joining the neck and body, which were made separately. Many vessels of the same type, but with a simple flared body instead of this rather squat shape, were made during the Parthian dynasty.

We have several specimens of handled vessels made during the Sassanian dynasty. One is a carafe said to have been found in Qazvin, Gilan Province, and now in the Teheran Archaeological Museum (fig. 56). It was made of opaque white glass, but the entire surface is now covered with a beautiful efflorescence. The lip is pointed, and the rim is attached directly to the body; the vessel does not have a constricted neck as seen in works of the Parthian dynasty. The handle is much longer, as well, stretching from the rim to the lower part of the body. As seen in this example, there is usually a thumb rest at the top of the handle, a device to prevent the vessel from slipping.

The handled vessels of the Sassanian dynasty, such as the one shown in plate 29, are characterized by the flowing contour of the vessel from the rim to the body; those of the early Islamic period usually have a beautifully curved line from the rim through the neck to the body, as seen in the ewer illustrated in plate 64. In works of the Sassanian dynasty (pl. 29, fig. 56) the constricted neck is joined to the body directly. In this respect the vessels resemble metalware. This is one way in which Sassanian works differ greatly from those of the subsequent Islamic period, though both types were made by blowing.

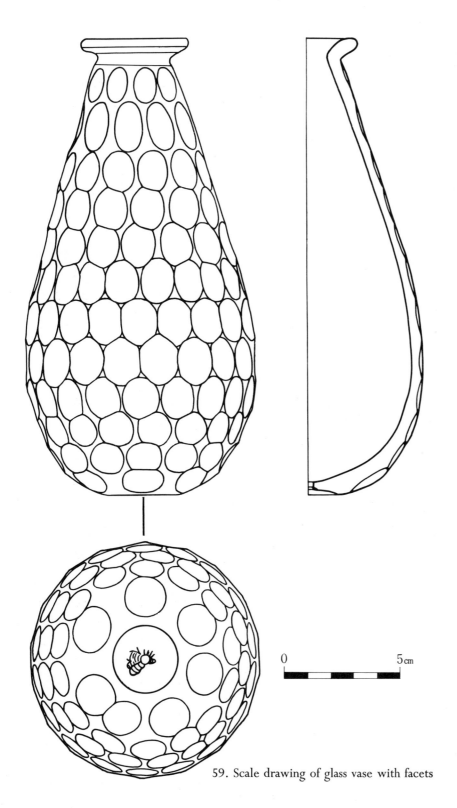

59. Scale drawing of glass vase with facets

No Sassanian-type works have yet been found in the course of scientifically conducted excavations. However, a vessel resembling a glass pitcher is held by the Persian fertility goddess Anahita in the relief carved in the Taq-i-Bustan cave (fig. 57). The pitcher is at the right edge of a scene depicting the investiture of Khosru II of Persia in 590, carved on the inner wall of a cave near Kermanshah in the Zagros Mountains in the Iranian highlands. The wavelike pattern on the vessel is somewhat unusual, but the carving can be taken as evidence of the existence of pitchers in the Iranian highlands during the late sixth century.

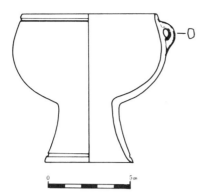

60. Goblet-shaped earthenware vessel with handle from Ghalekuti A

61. Earthenware oven, a mortuary vessel

Among the Shōsō-in treasures is a transparent glass carafe (fig. 58), of the type known in Japan as *kohei*. (Literally meaning "Persian vase," *kohei* refers to a metal or pottery vessel with a slender neck, a globular body, and a spout shaped like the head of a phoenix. It was used at court banquets.) The curvature from rim to body indicates that it was made in the early Islamic period rather than during the Sassanian dynasty. It was of course made in the Iranian highlands and taken to Japan via China.

VASES WITH CIRCULAR FACETS   The glass vase in plate 30 and figure 59 is said to have been found in a tomb in Gilan dating to the Sassanian dynasty. It was taken to Japan around 1961. As far as I know, only four pieces of this kind have been discovered.

The vase has a globular body narrowing upward to the rim, creating a teardrop shape. It is made of pale green thick translucent glass. There are twelve horizontal rows of circular facets on the body and seven circular facets around a large circular facet in the center of the base, executed in the same manner as seen on type I-A bowls.

A most interesting feature is a hole, about .4 cm. in diameter, perforating the vessel in the center of the facet on the base. There are scratches around the hole, and cracks running from it to the edges of the facet. There is also some shell-like flaking around the hole. These marks suggest that the hole was made after the vase was completed. What, then, is the explanation of the hole?

It is possible, though improbable, that the hole was made so the vessel could be used as a filter. However, the vessel's small capacity and the fact that there is only one hole make the vase unsuitable for filtering. Furthermore, elegant, decorative facets would not be expected on so humble and utilitarian an object as a filter. Far more probably, the vase was perforated for a religious or magical reason.

There is no universally accepted explanation of why people in the ancient world buried various objects, including deliberately perforated or broken objects and fragments of objects, with the dead. One theory is that life after death was thought of as similar to life on earth, hence the dead would need their worldly artifacts. Another explanation has it that the belongings of the dead were believed to have been contaminated by their owner's death and thus were no longer usable by the living. Yet another theory is that the graves in which such objects are found are the burial places of priests or shamans, whose belongings were believed to have retained their magical power even after their owner's death. The survivors, fearing that power, buried such objects with the owner.

Examples of mortuary vessels with perforated bases, or utili-

62. Fragment from the neck of a glass bottle *in situ*

tarian articles with similar holes, are found in graves throughout the ancient world, including the Americas. In the Iranian highlands, a 9-cm.-high, goblet-shaped earthenware vessel with a handle (fig. 60) was found in Ghalekuti tomb A-VII, estimated to date to about 700 B.C., in the Dailaman region. The bottom of the cup is completely missing, clearly indicating that the vessel was made specifically as a burial object. Numerous mortuary vessels, including an oven (fig. 61), an earthenware manger, and small bronze vessels, have been uncovered in this region.

Burial ornaments consisting of a pair of gold earrings, a bronze earpick, and a fragment of the neck of a glass bottle (fig. 62), all placed together upon a bronze hand mirror, were excavated from Noruz-mahale tomb D-IV, also in the Dailaman region. These pieces were discovered along with a mosaic glass bead (fig. 63) and a glass spinning whorl. This tomb has been estimated to be of the Parthian dynasty. It should be noted that no fragments except the single piece from the neck of the bottle were found in the tomb. It is presumed that the bottle was broken outside the tomb at the time of the burial and only the one fragment from the neck interred with the dead. The custom of breaking vessels and including a broken piece with other burial goods was common in the ancient world.

63. Mosaic glass bead from Noruz-mahale

As the vase shown in plate 30 was found in Gilan, reportedly in a Sassanian tomb, and as there are indications that the hole was made after the vessel was completed, it is reasonable to conclude that the hole was made at the time of burying the vase. This vessel, and other examples cited, confirm that the custom of burying mortuary vessels, and of perforating or breaking functional vessels to be buried with the dead, existed in Gilan.

64. Ointment bottle with feathered decoration from Ghalekuti I

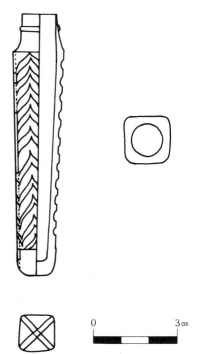

0   3 cm

65. Scale drawing of the bottle in figure 64

Other aspects of the globular vase call for further study. Did this type of vessel imitate the form of vessels made of materials other than glass, such as stoneware? Did the shape represent a continuation of an older traditional one? Did it originate in the bordering Roman world? At present, no similar vessels, from which its origin and tradition might be inferred, have been found. In any event, there is no question that this piece was made in the Iranian highlands in the Sassanian dynasty during the period that the concave-facet technique flourished.[17]

CORE-MOLDED GLASS Core-molding is thought to be the oldest method of making glass vessels. Briefly, the core was prepared by wrapping rags or caking mud around the end of a metal rod that had approximately the desired diameter of the mouth of the vessel to be made. The core was then dipped in molten glass, which adhered to it and set around it, forming a vessel. To decorate the vessel, strings of different-colored glass were wound around it before it had completely set, and a feathered pattern was created by combing the strings up and down. The core-molding technique flourished especially during the Eighteenth Dynasty in Egypt (1570–c. 1342 B.C.), and numerous small objects, such as cups, ointment bottles, and vials, were made at that time. Recent research has found that the core-molding method was used in Mesopotamia at about the same time as in Egypt.

Core-molded glass was found in Ghalekuti tomb I-V in the Dailaman region. The example illustrated in figures 64 and 65 is a slender rectangular ointment bottle with a cylindrical neck made separately and attached. It had already been broken into three pieces when it was discovered; furthermore, it was impossible to determine the original color, as the glass had completely effloresced. The rim section has a very thin neck with a string of yellow glass wound around the middle. The surface is covered with a feathered pattern. The interior space is a cylinder that gradually narrows toward the base. The edges of the four sides are decorated with yellow glass strings like the one around the neck. The strings along the sides extend to the base and cross it diagonally.

Judging from the age of the other burial goods in Ghalekuti tomb I-V, this ointment bottle was made around the fourth or third century B.C. Because imports from the eastern Mediterranean coastal region were discovered with it, it is assumed that the vessel was imported from the Levant. A few similar pieces, including those in plate 32, have been found in Gilan.

Another ointment bottle (pl. 31, fig. 66) was found with this specimen. It is of pale green glass with a flared lip and a long cylindrical body decorated with a thin glass string trailed in a spiral. This bottle was also made by the core-molding method and probably also came from the Levant.[18]

Ornaments and Other Objects

In addition to glass vessels of the Partho-Sassanian period found in the Iranian highlands, other glass artifacts, especially ornaments, deserve mention.

BEADS Beads were used for jewelry in the Iranian highlands as long ago as the early farming culture, but it was only during the Parthian dynasty that they became very common. They must also have been used during the succeeding Sassanian dynasty, but as yet we have no evidence to corroborate this assumption.

It is more difficult to determine when and where the numerous glass beads found in tombs of the Parthian dynasty in Persia were made than to determine the same for glass vessels. I will attempt to date some of these beads, but will concern myself only with those found in the course of scientific excavation. However, partly because I have not done sufficient personal research, I will withhold opinion on the place of manufacture. On this difficult matter, it must be remembered that jewelry was made to be worn, hence was carried about from place to place even more frequently than were other glass objects.

The glass beads found by archaeologists may be grouped into two chronological categories: those from the fourth to the first century B.C. and those from the first century B.C. to the third century A.D.

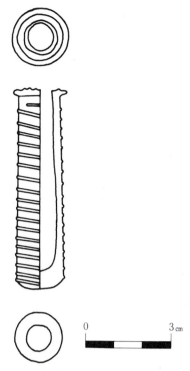

66. Scale drawing of an ointment bottle decorated with trailed glass strings from Ghalekuti I

1. *Glass beads of the fourth to first century B.C.* This corresponds roughly to the late Achaemenid and early Parthian dynasties if we divide the latter into two halves at about the time of Christ. The following types of glass beads have been found in tombs believed to date from the early period: eye beads, round beads with a white disk in the middle, tangerine-shaped beads, and tube beads made of glass paste.

Eye beads. An eye-bead necklace (pls. 39, 40) was found in Ghalekuti tomb I-V in Gilan, where the core-molded ointment bottles were found. These eye beads are of three varieties: round beads, round beads flattened at top and bottom, and smaller beads of the first two varieties. The beads have a common background color, dark blue, and are inlaid with eyes consisting of concentric circles of white and dark blue glass. The diameters of the beads vary from approximately 1.3 cm. to .6 cm.

Two other varieties of eye beads were found in Ghalekuti tomb II-III. One has the blue background color, but each inlaid eye is formed of concentric circles of yellow, blue, white, and blue glass. (An example is shown at the far left of the top row of plate 45.) The other type has a reddish brown background, and each inlaid eye comprises concentric circles of yellow, blue, white, and blue (pl. 46 top row, far left); vari-

57

ous other kinds of eye beads have also been unearthed (pls. 45, 46). Examples of eye beads found at various Middle Eastern sites are discussed below.

(A) An eye bead made of glass paste was found in a subterranean shaft grave in tomb T-39 at Gibeon in the Palestine region. This bead has a matte yellow ground, and the inlaid eye is green and white. The excavator dates tomb T-39 to period I to II of the middle Bronze Age.[19]

(B) Eye beads made of glass paste were found in a shaft grave of tomb 24 excavated at 'Atlit in Palestine. One bead is inlaid with a blue eye on a white background, one with a blue and white eye on a yellow background, and one with a white eye on a dark blue background. The excavator estimates the tomb to be of the fourth century B.C.[20]

(C) Eye beads made of glass paste were also found in a shaft grave in tomb 21f at 'Atlit. One bead is inlaid with a dark blue eye on a pale blue background, another with a dark blue eye on a yellow background. The excavator also dates this tomb to the fourth century B.C.[21]

(D) An eye bead inlaid with a dark blue and white eye on a pale blue ground was excavated from stratum II of Tell Abu Hawām in Palestine. The excavator thinks stratum II to be of the sixth to fourth century B.C.[22]

(E) Two eye beads were found at Persepolis. One is inlaid with a gray line on a white ground, and its center is purplish red. The other is inlaid with a white line on a bright yellowish brown ground. Both are artifacts of the sixth to fourth century B.C.[23]

(F) Four eye beads were found in a tomb on Ghalekuti hill I in Gilan. The tombs in this area are estimated to be of the late Bronze Age or early Iron Age, or the early first millennium B.C. I understand that these beads have effloresced badly, making it difficult to determine the original color of the glass.[24]

Eye beads have also been discovered all the way from southern Russia through Eastern Europe to Western Europe, including some that are of exactly the same type as those found in the Middle East, especially those from Gilan. These beads are inlaid with yellow eyes on a dark blue ground or with yellow eyes on a green ground (see the second cluster of beads from the right in the second row from the top in plate 46). In East Asia, numerous eye beads found at the Chin Ts'un site at Loyang in Honan Province, China, belong to China's Warring States period (480–221 B.C.) and are dated to around the third century B.C.

In general, it can be said that the eye beads found in the Middle East are mostly of the sixth to fourth century B.C., although some of those found in Gilan may date back as far as the early first millennium.

Round beads with a white disk in the middle. This type of bead is made by joining two amber-colored glass hemispheres to a white glass disk so that the finished bead consists of stripes of amber, white, and amber glass (fig. 67). The beads were made either by joining together pieces with holes in them or by coiling glass around a rod. Two beads of this type were recovered from Ghalekuti tomb II-III and are estimated to be of the fourth to third century B.C. Beads similar to these are shown in the middle row of plate 48.

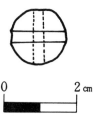

67. Round bead with a white disk in the middle (actual size)

Tangerine-shaped beads. These beads are made of clear, pale blue glass. The top and bottom of the beads are flattened, and they somewhat resemble a tangerine in shape, with evenly spaced fluting on the surface. Numerous beads of this type were found in Ghalekuti tomb I-V, but they disintegrated while being excavated, most of them losing their original shape entirely (a fact not mentioned in the excavators' report). However, examples of this type of bead are shown at the extreme right and second from the right in the middle row of plate 50.

Tube beads made of glass paste. These spindle-shaped beads are long and narrow, bulging in the middle and tapering to either end. The surface has a pattern resembling that of onyx, and both ends have green or yellow glass bands. These beads were also excavated from Ghalekuti tomb I-V (the three pieces at the left, pl. 52) and are estimated to have been made in the fourth or third century B.C.

68. Pumpkin bead (actual size)

2. *Glass beads of the first to third century A.D.* This period corresponds to the late Parthian dynasty. Types of beads from this period found at Hassani-mahale and Noruz-mahale in the Dailaman region are listed below (it should be noted that the late Parthian dynasty is characterized by a complete lack of eye beads): joined small beads, flat lozenge-shaped beads, mosaic beads, cut-glass beads, twisted beads, tube beads, and pumpkin beads.

Joined small beads. These small, round, milky white beads joined in pairs were found in Noruz-mahale tomb B-IV.

Mosaic beads. A single fragmented example (later pieced together) was found in Noruz-mahale tomb D-IV (see the beads in the second row from the bottom in plate 47).

Cut-glass beads. A blue cut-glass bead was found at Noruz-mahale.

Twisted beads. These green and blue beads were found in Noruz-mahale tomb D-IV.

Tube beads. These blue beads with a square cross section and a round hole were found in Hassani-mahale tomb IV.

Pumpkin beads. These are amber-colored and shaped somewhat like a pumpkin (fig. 68). They were excavated from Hassani-mahale tomb VII.

A necklace of small dark blue and white glass beads (diameter .5 cm.) was found in Hassani-mahale tomb VII. From their position at the time of excavation it was determined that one white bead and four dark blue beads had been strung alternately (fig. 69).

RINGS AND PENDANTS   A glass ring, consisting of a thin white spiral band wound around a yellowish brown background and with a pale yellow glass bead set in the center of the ring (fig. 70) was found in Khoramrud tomb A-IV, thought to date to the first to third century A.D. A copper ring with a glass setting (fig. 71) was found in Hassani-mahale tomb IV, which is believed to be of the same period. This ring's setting is carved with an animal motif. Another common Parthian motif, that of figures from Greco-Roman mythology, is carved on the light brown glass setting of the copper ring shown in plate 54. In addition to rings, pendants were common. Those shown in plate 59 have mold-pressed patterns with animal motifs.

SPINNING WHORLS   Three dark blue glass spinning whorls were found in Hassani-mahale tomb IV. These conical whorls were made by trailing glass strings in a spiral; however, the whorl was usually finished as a truncated cone. Fusing of the glass is easily discernible at the base, and air bubbles remain at the bonded surfaces of some specimens. On one of the whorls from Hassani-mahale, a white glass string is used to achieve a striped effect against the dark blue background. The same type of whorl was found in Noruz-mahale tomb D-IV.

Until the early Parthian dynasty, earthenware whorls were predominant, but earthenware, bone, and glass all seem to have been used for making spinning whorls beginning soon after the time of Christ.

GAME PIECES   It is uncertain whether any game comparable to chess existed in the Iranian highlands during the late Parthian dynasty, but artifacts presumed to have been used as pieces in some sort of board game have been found. The objects shown in plate 51, except for those at either end, are said to have been found in Gilan in a set of twenty-four pieces: twelve pieces with white dots on a dark blue ground, and twelve with yellow dots on a green ground. They can be dated to the first to third century.

The counters were made by preparing a core of opaque white glass, which was coated with a layer of mosaic glass about .1 cm. thick. The dots become increasingly distorted toward the base of the piece, where the surface is almost vertical, showing how the coating ran. A set of twenty-four similar pieces, found in England and estimated to date to the latter half of the first century B.C., is in the British Museum.[25]

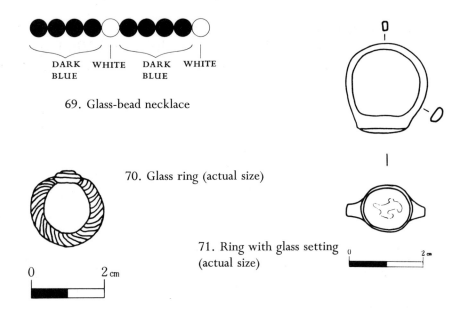

DARK WHITE DARK WHITE
BLUE   BLUE

69. Glass-bead necklace

70. Glass ring (actual size)

71. Ring with glass setting
(actual size)

0   2 cm

0   2 cm

In addition to the objects discussed above, many glass figurines of both humans and animals have been found, but most belong to the Islamic period. The animal figurine shown in plate 38, a work of the late Parthian dynasty from Gilan, is an extremely rare example from this early time. The efflorescence shows characteristics peculiar to glass from Gilan.

3 The Islamic Period

Glassware of the Islamic period, which began in the seventh to eighth century, developed in the context of the cultural legacy of the Eastern Roman (Byzantine) Empire and the Partho-Sassanian period of Persia. It had been thought that the glass objects commonly referred to as being of the Islamic period were made only in Egypt, Syria, and Mesopotamia. However, it is noteworthy that in recent years numerous glass objects attributed to the Islamic period have been found at Ray, Gurgan, and Nishapur in the Iranian highlands, as well as Samarkand. As a result of scientific excavations, it is now known that glass vessels were made from the ninth century onward in Nishapur and Samarkand.

The glassmaking techniques used in the Iranian highlands during the Islamic period were the traditional mold-blowing method, used to make thick glass since the Partho-Sassanian period, and the free-blowing method for producing thin glass, as seen in Syrian glassware. Great beauty of shape is possible with the free-blowing method, which reached its culmination during the Islamic period.

A variety of decorative techniques was used, including some unique to the period. The techniques include ornamentation by cutting, ornamentation with trailed strings, feathered ornamentation, mold-pressed ornamentation, and medallion application.

Ornamentation by cutting. This technique had been in use since the Partho-Sassanian period. It is believed to have continued to be fashionable in the Iranian highlands during the Islamic period, with the production of cut glass flourishing especially in Nishapur.

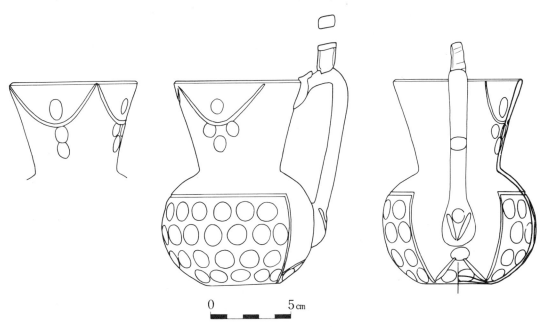

72. Scale drawing of wide-mouthed pitcher

The decoration on the narrow-necked ninth-century ointment bottle shown in plate 71 consists of the most traditional type of concave circular facets. However, in the early Islamic period the most common type of faceted ornamentation was circular planed facets having a U-shaped cross section, cut by the up-and-down motion of a grindstone (pls. 79, 80). Frequently the facets made by this method are oval. The corners of the neck on many narrow-necked ointment bottles, a form peculiar to the early Islamic period, were planed off.

The wide-mouthed ninth-century pitchers shown in plates 68 and 70 and the one illustrated in plate 69 and figure 72 have a shape characteristic of the early Islamic period. It is interesting to note that the entire surface of the pitcher shown in plate 69 and figure 72 is covered with a beautiful efflorescence and the circular facets on the body are finished like frosted glass. Gradually the cut ornamentation of the early Islamic period went out of style and was replaced by cut decorations with flat surfaces, achieved by vertical movements of the grindstone.

Ornamentation with trailed strings. This decorative technique was frequently used to embellish glass vessels of the Syrian type made by free-blowing. Glass strings of various colors were trailed many times over the vessel's body or applied so as to achieve a wavelike pattern. This technique was commonly used to decorate such objects as narrow-necked ointment bottles (pl. 76).

Feathered ornamentation. The technique of feathering to decorate core-molded glass is traceable to ancient Egypt and Phoenicia. The technique regained popularity in the Islamic period and continued in use until around the twelfth century. Many of the works decorated by this technique are small objects, such as ointment vases (pl. 81 left), ointment bottles, and bird figurines, probably because of the technical limitations of the method itself.

Mold-pressed ornamentation. This decorative technique was also carried over from the Partho-Sassanian period (pls. 61–63, 70, 73–75). The vessel shown in plate 61, decorated with raised patterns on both the exterior and the interior surfaces, is a remarkable example of a technique considered to be peculiar to the early Islamic period.

Medallion application. This method involves application of pattern molds to the object to be embellished. It was frequently used to decorate earthenware during the Sassanian dynasty. The method was used on relatively small glass vessels during the late Sassanian dynasty and the early Islamic period (pls. 81 right, 82).

Luster, gilding, and enameling were other common decorative techniques in the Islamic period, but they do not appear to have been much used in the Iranian highlands.

Following the thirteenth-century Mongol invasion and subsequent conquest of Persia, pottery manufacture flourished in the Iranian highlands but glassmaking declined markedly. However, during the rule of Shah 'Abbas I (1587–1629) glasswork was revived in the highlands, with Shiraz as its center. The rosewater sprinkler in plate 88 is representative of the glassware made in Shiraz.

Notes

1. EARLY GLASS

1. E. Porada, *Tchoga Zanbil*, vol. 4, *Mémoires de la délégation archéologique en Iran* 42 (Paris: 1970).

2. Roman Ghirshman, "The Elamite Levels at Susa and Their Chronological Significance," *American Journal of Archaeology* 74, no. 3 (1970): 225.

3. G. Herrmann, "Lapis Lazuli: The Early Phases of Its Trade," *Iraq* 30, pt. 1 (1968): 21–27.

4. Ezat O. Negahban, *A Preliminary Report on Marlik Excavation, Rudbar, 1961–1962* (Teheran: 1964).

5. Axel von Saldern, "Mosaic Glass from Hasanlu, Marlik, and Tell al-Rimah," *Journal of Glass Studies* 8 (1966).

6. Ibid., pp. 10–12.

7. Sachiko Oda, *Chemical Study on the Material of Beads from the Ghalekuti I Site, Dailaman I*, Tokyo University Iraq-Iran Archaeological Expedition Report 6 (Tokyo: 1965).

8. E. Herzfeld, "Eine Silberschussel Artaxerxes I," *Archaeologische Mitteilungen aus Iran* 7 (Berlin: 1935).

9. E. F. Schmidt, *Persepolis II* (Chicago: 1957), p. 92.

10. Poul Fossing, "Drinking Bowls of Glass and Metal from the Achaemenian Times," *Berytus* 4, fasc. 2 (Copenhagen: 1937).

11. Axel von Saldern, "Achaemenid and Sassanian Cut Glass," *Ars Orientalis* 5 (1963).

12. Dan Barag, "An Unpublished Achaemenid Cut Glass Bowl from Nippur," *Journal of Glass Studies* 10 (1968).

13. Andrew Oliver, "Persian Export Glass," *Journal of Glass Studies* 12 (1970).

2. THE PARTHO-SASSANIAN PERIOD

1. Toshihiko Sono and Shinji Fukai, *Dailaman III 1964*, Tokyo University Iraq-Iran Archaeological Expedition Report 8 (Tokyo: 1968).

2. Ibid.

3. Ibid.

4. Namio Egami, Shinji Fukai, and Seiichi Masuda, *Dailaman II 1960*, Tokyo University Iraq-Iran Archaeological Expedition Report 7 (Tokyo: 1966).

5. Ibid.

6. Axel von Saldern, "Achaemenid and Sassanian Cut Glass," *Ars Orientalis* 5 (1963): 10.

7. Shōsō-in Office, *Shōsō-in no garasu* [Glass objects in the Shōsō-in] (Tokyo: 1965).

8. Shinji Fukai, "Shōsō-in hōmotsu haku-ruriwan kō" [Notes on the glass bowl in the Shōsō-in treasury], *Kokka*, no. 812 (November 1959).

9. Aurel Stein, *The Thousand Buddhas* (London: 1921), p. 43, pl. 29.

10. *Shōsō-in no garasu*, p. 10.

11. Shinji Fukai, *Perushia kobijutsu kenkyū* [Study of Iranian art and archaeology] (Tokyo: 1968), pp. 11–12.

12. Nara Prefecture Board of Education, *Yamato Niizawa Senzuka—chōsa gaihō, Shōwa 37, 38 nendo* [Report of surveys of the Yamato Niizawa Senzuka tombs, 1962, 1963] (Nara: 1963).

13. Committee to Restore Munakata Shrine, *Okinoshima—Munakata Jinja Okitsumiya saishi iseki* [Okinoshima—the Okitsumiya religious ruins of Munakata Shrine] (1958), pp. 221–23.

14. Shinji Fukai, "Okinoshima shutsudo ruriwan dampen kō" [Notes on the fragments of a glass bowl found on Okinoshima], *Tōyō bunka kenkyūjō kiyō* [Bulletin of the Institute of Oriental Culture] 27 (March 1962).

15. D. B. Harden, "Excavations at Kish and Barghuthiat 1933," *Iraq* 1, pt. 2 (1934), fig. 4, pls. 10, 11; fig. 5, pls. 12, 13.

16. R. W. Smith, "New Finds of Ancient Glass in North Africa," *Ars Orientalis* 2 (1957): 100.

17. Shinji Fukai, "Kiriko sōshoku ruritsubo—Gilan-shū shutsudo kiriko sōshoku ruritsubo ni kansuru shiron" [A glass vase with facet decoration—essay on a glass vase with facet decoration found in Gilan Province], *Tōyō bunka kenkyūjō kiyō* [Bulletin of the Institute of Oriental Culture] 29 (1963).

18. Shinji Fukai, "Dailaman chihō shutsudo no koa-garasu" [Core-molded glass excavated in the Dailaman region], *Tōyō bunka kenkyūjō kiyō* [Bulletin of the Institute of Oriental Culture] 56 (1972).

19. James B. Pritchard, *The Bronze Age Cemetery at Gibeon* (University Museum, University of Pennsylvania: 1963), p. 48, pl. 72.

20. C. N. Johns, "Excavations at 'Atlit (1930): The Southeastern Cemetery," *Quarterly of the Department of Antiquities in Palestine* 2, nos. 2, 3 (1932), p. 97, pl. 33.

21. Ibid., pp. 52, 80; pls. 25, 36.

22. R. W. Hamilton, "Excavations at Tell Abu Hawām," *Quarterly of the Department of Antiquities in Palestine* 4, nos. 1, 2 (1934), pp. 2–5, 18; pl. 34.

23. E. F. Schmidt, *Persepolis II* (Chicago: 1957), pl. 43 (11, 12).

24. Sachiko Oda, *Chemical Study on the Material of Beads from the Ghale-kuti I Site, Dailaman I*, Tokyo University Iraq-Iran Archaeological Expedition Report 6 (Tokyo: 1965), pp. 39–47.

25. British Museum, *Masterpieces of Glass* (London: 1968), p. 35.

COLOR PLATES AND COMMENTARIES

1. Bowl with circular facets. Gilan Province. 3rd–7th century. Height 8.1 cm., diameter 11.4 cm. Private collection, Kyoto.

A bowl with a slightly constricted rim, made of light brown translucent glass containing many air bubbles.

1

2. Bowl with circular facets. Gilan Province. 3rd–7th century. Height 8 cm., diameter 10.7 cm. Private collection, Tokyo.

A thick bowl of light brown translucent glass containing many air bubbles. There are thirteen circular facets in each of the top two rows, and seven in the bottom row ringing a large circular facet cut into the base.

3. Bowl with circular facets. Gilan Province. 3rd–7th century. Height 8 cm., diameter 10.7 cm. Private collection, Tokyo.

A bowl with a vertical rim, made of light brown opaque glass containing many air bubbles. There are fourteen circular facets in the top row, fifteen in the second, fourteen in the third, seven slightly larger facets in the bottom row, and a large circular facet at the base.

2

3

4. Bowl with circular facets. Gilan Province. 3rd–7th century. Height 8.4 cm., diameter 9.8 cm. Private collection, Tokyo.

A bowl with a slightly constricted rim, made of light brown translucent glass containing many air bubbles. There are twenty-three circular facets in each of the first six rows, and seven slightly larger facets in the lowest row ringing one large circular facet cut into the base. The seven facets in the lowest row have spaces between them, each space containing a double facet.

5. Bowl with wave pattern. Gilan Province. 3rd–7th century. Height 8.2 cm., diameter 11.1 cm. Private collection, Tokyo.

A bowl with a vertical rim, made of pale green opaque glass containing many air bubbles. The rim section is embellished with a wide incised groove. There are twenty-four square facets below the incised line. Two rows of double arcs on the body create a wave pattern. There is another incised groove near the base, with five oval facets inside the groove, surrounding a circular facet at the base.

4

5

6. Bowl with facets. Gilan Province. 1st–3rd century. Height 8.7 cm., diameter 12 cm. Private collection, Tokyo.

A bowl with a thick body and a thin outward-curving rim, made of pale green glass containing many air bubbles. There is a circular facet at the base, with ten oval facets in the upper row and five oval facets in the lower row.

7. Bowl with circular facets. Gilan Province. 1st–3rd century. Height 8.1 cm., diameter 11.9 cm. Private collection, Tokyo.

A bowl with an outward-curving rim like that shown in plate 6, made of pale green glass containing many air bubbles. There are eight circular facets just below the middle of the body and five more circular facets surrounding a circular facet at the base.

6

7

8. Bowl with ornamental blobs. Gilan Province. 3rd–5th century. Height 8.3 cm., diameter 11 cm. Private collection, Tokyo.

A vessel of transparent glass, with a rim that curves outward. Blobs of dark blue glass ring the middle of the body.

9. Bowl with circular facets. Gilan Province. 3rd–7th century. Height 6.8 cm., diameter 9.1 cm. Private collection, Tokyo.

A bowl of white opaque glass, with a distinctly constricted neck and a rim that turns outward. There are numerous small circular facets on the body. This vessel is very similar to a glass bowl found in one of the Nii-zawa Senzuka tombs in Kashiwabara, Nara Prefecture.

8

9

10. Cup with ornamental protrusions. Gilan Province. 1st–3rd century. Height 9.4 cm., diameter 10.3 cm. Private collection, Tokyo.

A vessel of pale green glass containing many air bubbles. There are large ornamental protrusions below the rim. The body is decorated with regularly spaced glass strings of the same color trailed around it.

10

11. Bowl with facets in relief. Gilan Province. 3rd–4th century. Height 8 cm., diameter 9.5 cm. Private collection, Tokyo.

A footed bowl with a slightly constricted rim, made of pale green opaque glass. There are seven circular facets cut in relief in the upper row and seven fingertip-sized, almond-shaped molded relief facets in the lower row. Each facet has a concave surface.

11

12. Bowl with double circular facets. Gilan Province. 6th century. Height 8 cm., diameter 10.3 cm. Private collection, Tokyo.

A bowl with a slightly constricted rim and a double-tiered foot, made of light brown opaque glass. There are six evenly spaced double circular facets on the body.

12

13. Bowl with double circular facets. Gilan Province. 6th century. Height 8 cm., diameter 11.3 cm. Private collection, Osaka.

A footed bowl with a slightly constricted rim, made of light brown opaque glass. There are two rows of six double circular facets.

13

14. Footed bowl with ornamental protrusions. Gilan Province. 1st–3rd century. Height 7.7 cm., diameter 9.6 cm. Collection of Okayama Gakuen, Okayama.

A footed bowl with a constricted rim, made of pale green opaque glass containing many air bubbles.

14

15. Bowl with ornamental protrusions. Gilan Province. 1st–3rd century. Height 8.5 cm., diameter 10.3 cm. Collection of Saburō Matsumoto, Tokyo.

A bowl with a bulging body and a rim curving outward like that of an inverted bell, made of pale green glass containing many air bubbles. There are large ornamental protrusions on the bulging midsection of the body and one row of small protrusions below them. Small protrusions that function as feet surround a pontil mark in the center of the base.

16. Bowl with mold-pressed decoration (base shown). Gilan Province. 1st–3rd century. Height 7.4 cm., diameter 10.1 cm. Private collection, Tokyo.

A footed bowl with a constricted rim, made of pale green opaque glass containing many air bubbles. The surface is decorated with mold-pressed serpentine patterns.

15

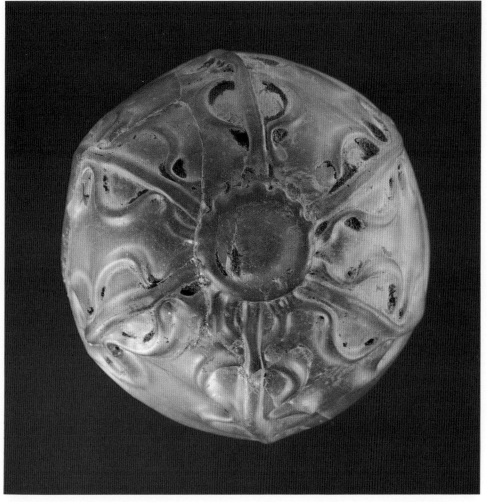

16

17. Footed cup (left) and bowl (right). Gilan Province. 1st–3rd century. Left: height 5.6 cm., diameter 9.6 cm. Right: height 4.4 cm., diameter 9.4 cm. Private collection, Nagoya.

The footed cup is made of pale green glass containing many air bubbles, and has a pontil mark at the base. The foot and the body were made separately, then joined. The bowl is made of thick purple glass and also has a pontil mark at the base. This vessel's use is unknown.

17

18. Stemmed goblet with cut decoration. Gilan Province. 1st–3rd century. Height 29.3 cm., diameter 9.8 cm. Collection of Saburō Matsumoto, Tokyo.

A stemmed goblet of pale green translucent glass that has effloresced. The foot and body are one piece. There are three rows of concave oval facets, with eleven facets in the top row, ten in the middle row, and ten in the bottom row. Vertical lines are incised between the rows of oval facets, with thirty-one lines in the upper row and thirty in the lower. In addition to these cut decorations, the goblet is decorated with twelve incised horizontal lines.

18

19. Footed goblet with cut decoration. Gilan Province. 3rd–7th century. Height 11.5 cm., diameter 12 cm. Collection of Okayama Gakuen, Okayama.

A footed goblet of pale green translucent glass. The foot is of a piece with the goblet. Below the rim are incised twenty-five contiguous arcs. The motif is repeated on the midsection, where there are twenty-one arcs, and again at the bottom, where there are thirteen. There are ten circular facets on the upper half of the vessel and seven on the lower half.

19

20. Stemmed goblet with facets. Gilan Province. 5th–7th century. Height 16.7 cm., diameter 10.5 cm. Private collection, Tokyo.
    A stemmed, footed goblet of light brown translucent glass that has effloresced. The foot was made separately, then joined to the goblet.

20

21. Conical beaker with ornamental blobs. Gilan Province. 3rd–5th century. Height 14.4 cm., diameter 6.6 cm. Private collection, Tokyo.

A rhyton-shaped vessel of fairly thick clear glass. Twenty-one blobs of blue glass encircle the vessel, and there are incised lines around the rim and above and below the decorative blobs.

22. Conical beaker with ornamental blobs. Gilan Province. 3rd–5th century. Height 19.1 cm., diameter 9.2 cm. Private collection, Tokyo.

A rhyton-shaped vessel of thin white translucent glass. On the upper half are two groups of five blobs of blue glass, arranged to form two inverted triangles opposite each other, with two larger blobs of blue glass between the triangles. The rim is finished in an unusual fashion: it curves outward and then turns upward. There are horizontal incised lines above and below the blobs.

22

21

23. Cup with facets. Gilan Province. 3rd–5th century. Height 7.2 cm., diameter 6.7 cm. Collection of Tenri Museum.

An almost conical vessel of pale yellow translucent glass. There are incised lines near the rim and slightly below the middle of the vessel.

24. Flask with spout at the bottom. Gilan Province. 1st–3rd century. Height 18.4 cm. Private collection, Kyoto.

A vessel made of pale green glass. The entire surface is covered with efflorescence and petrified mud, making it difficult to recognize the mold-pressed pattern. The spout at the bottom is adopted from the rhyton.

23   24

25. Dish with circular facets (base shown). Gilan Province. 5th–7th century. Height 5 cm., diameter 17.3 cm. Private collection, Tokyo.

Because the dish has effloresced badly, it is difficult to comment on the quality of the glass. There are seven circular facets around the large circular facet in the center of the base, twelve circular facets in the second row, twenty-three hexagonal facets in the third row, and twenty-three circular facets in the top row. The same type of dish has been found at Kish in southern Mesopotamia.

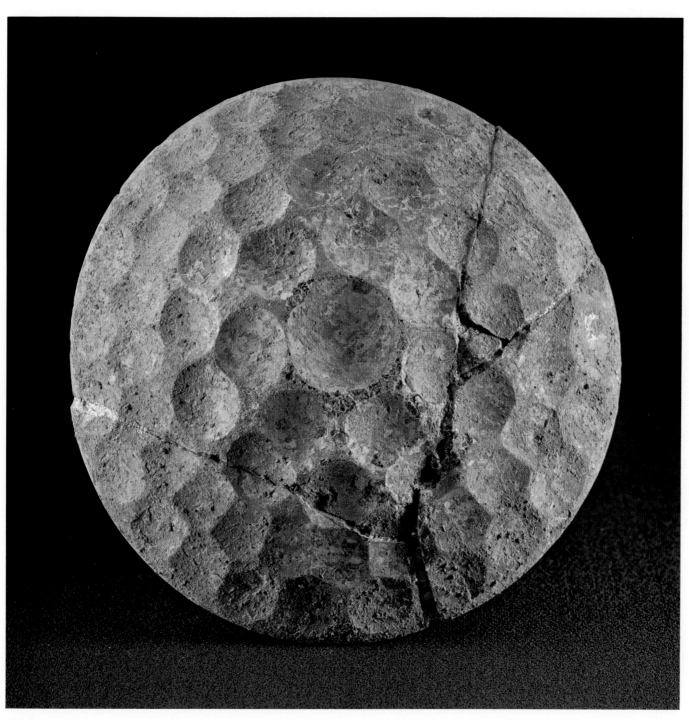

25

26. Dish with double circular facets (base shown). Gilan Province. 5th–7th century. Height 4.7 cm., diameter 14.8 cm. Private collection, Tokyo.

A dish with an outward-turned rim, made of pale green translucent glass. There are four circular facets surrounding a double facet in the center of the base. The part of the rim that turns outward is embellished with incised lines.

27. Dish with circular facets in relief (base shown). Gilan Province. 5th–7th century. Diameter 13.3 cm. Private collection, Tokyo.

A dish of pale green translucent glass that has effloresced. There is a circular facet in relief (diameter 3.7 cm.), with a central ornamental protrusion, at the base and six circular facets in relief, with a protrusion in the middle of each, spaced regularly around it. In addition, there are six ornamental protrusions near the lip in the spaces between the six facets.

26

27

28. Pitcher. Gilan Province. 1st–3rd century. Height 10.4 cm. Private collection, Tokyo.

A pitcher with a rolled rim, made of translucent glass that has efflo-resced. A mark remains where the neck and body were joined when the vessel was made. There are vertical ribs on the body, which bulges toward the base, and a pontil mark in the center of the base.

28

29. Carafe. Gilan Province. 5th–7th century. Height 22.1 cm. Private collection, Tokyo.

A "*kohei*-form" carafe of thick white translucent glass, made by free-blowing. There is a pontil mark at the base.

29

30. Vase with facets. Gilan Province. 3rd–7th century. Height 19.4 cm. Private collection, Tokyo.

A teardrop-shaped vase made of thick pale green translucent glass. The surface is divided into twelve horizontal rows. There is one large circular facet at the base, with seven facets in the first row above the base, fourteen in the second row, seventeen in the third row, nineteen each in the fourth, fifth, sixth, and seventh rows, sixteen in the eighth row, fifteen in the ninth row, thirteen in the tenth row, ten in the eleventh row, and nine in the top row. A hole .4 cm. in diameter perforates the center of the base.

31. Ointment bottle. Ghalekuti tomb I-V, Dailaman, Gilan Province. 4th–2nd century B.C. Height 6.7 cm., diameter 1.9 cm. Collection of the Institute of Oriental Culture, Tokyo University.

A bottle of white opaque glass containing many air bubbles. The vessel is decorated with a glass string trailed around the body.

32. Ointment bottles. Gilan Province. 4th–2nd century B.C. Left: height 8.5 cm. Right: height 7.2 cm. Private collection, Tokyo.

Both of these long, narrow, rectangular bottles with short cylindrical necks are made of purple core-molded glass. The necks, which were made separately and then attached, are light brown or pale purple. Each bottle has the feathered decoration common in core-molded glass. The edges of the bottles where the four sides join are decorated with applied strings of yellow glass.

33. Vial. Gilan Province. 1st–3rd century. Height 12.2 cm. Private collection, Tokyo.

A vial of pale green glass that has effloresced to a golden color. There is a pontil mark at the base.

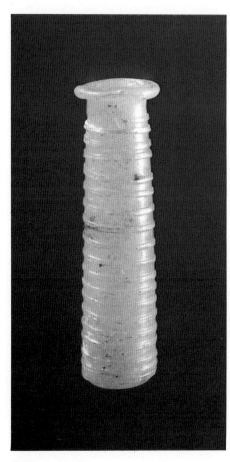

31

32

33

34. Ointment vase. Gilan Province. 3rd–7th century. Height 8.9 cm. Private collection, Tokyo.

A vase of thick green translucent glass, probably used to hold ointment. The same type of vessel has been found at Banbol in Pakistan.

35. Small vase with molded decoration. Gilan Province. 1st–3rd century. Height 6.6 cm. Private collection, Nagoya.

A vase of pale green translucent glass containing a few air bubbles. It has a molded relief design typical of the Parthian dynasty. Probably the vase was used to hold ointment.

34

35

36. Ointment bottle with oval facets in relief. Gilan Province. 1st–3rd century. Height 11.1 cm. Private collection, Nagoya.

A slender bottle of light brown translucent glass. The neck is in two tiers, with the edges planed. The body is widest in the middle, tapering to either end. There are three oval facets in relief on the middle portion of the body, while three more on the lower part of the body serve as feet.

37. Ointment vial. Gilan Province. 1st–3rd century. Height 11.8 cm., diameter at lip 3.9 cm. Collection of Okayama Gakuen, Okayama.

A vial of pale green translucent glass, with fluting on the body and rim section; the fluting on the rim is twisted slightly.

37

36

38. Animal figurine. Gilan Province. 1st–3rd century. Height 4.9 cm. Private collection, Tokyo.

The original color is indeterminable, as the entire surface has effloresced.

38

39, 40. Necklace. Ghalekuti tomb I-V, Dailaman, Gilan Province. 4th–2nd century B.C. Collection of the Institute of Oriental Culture, Tokyo University.

This piece was discovered in 1964 by the Tokyo University Iraq-Iran Archaeological Expedition. The sizes of the beads differ, but all are inlaid with white and dark blue eyes on a blue background.

39

40

41. Necklaces. Gilan Province. 4th–2nd century B.C. Private collection, Tokyo.

The necklace on the left contains various inlaid beads, while that on the right contains so-called sandwich beads and gold beads as well as inlaid beads.

41

42. Necklaces. Gilan Province. 4th–2nd century B.C. Private collection, Tokyo.

The necklace on the left is of ordinary inlaid beads, except that the eyes on the large bead in the center are applied, not inlaid. The small beads on the necklace on the right are of the same kind as those found at Persepolis.

43. Necklaces. Gilan Province. 1st–3rd century. Private collection, Tokyo.

The necklace on the left is of round, dark blue beads of the same kind as those found in Hassani-mahale tomb VII in the Dailaman region. The necklace on the right is of round, pale green beads.

44. Necklaces. Gilan Province. 1st–3rd century. Private collection, Tokyo.

Both necklaces are made of dark blue lozenge-shaped beads. Efflorescence has turned parts of the beads white.

45. Beads. Gilan Province. 4th–2nd century B.C. Private collection, Tokyo.

All the beads are inlaid except for those in the bottom row that have applied eyes.

45

46. Beads. Gilan Province. 4th–2nd century B.C. Private collection, Tokyo.

All the beads are inlaid except for those in the bottom row.

46

47. Beads. Gilan Province. 1st–3rd century. Private collection, Tokyo. The second row from the bottom contains mosaic beads.

47

48. Beads. Gilan Province. 1st–3rd century. Private collection, Tokyo.
In the middle row are beads with white glass sandwiched between colored glass.

48

49. Beads. Gilan Province. 4th–3rd century B.C. Private collection, Tokyo.

The middle row shows twisted beads, while the beads in the second row from the bottom are core-molded.

49

50. Beads. Gilan Province. 4th century B.C.–3rd century A.D. Private collection, Tokyo.

The second row from the top contains sandwich beads. The three beads on the right in the middle row are tangerine-shaped.

51. Game pieces. Gilan Province. 1st–3rd century. Private collection, Tokyo.

These objects do not have a hole in the center as beads do. Each is made of a core of white opaque glass coated with a layer of mosaic glass approximately .1 cm. thick. The objects may have been used as counters in a board game.

52. Tube beads of glass paste. Gilan Province. 4th–3rd century B.C. The three pieces on the left are in the collection of the Institute of Oriental Culture, Tokyo University. The two on the right are in a private collection, Tokyo.

Long spindle-shaped beads with onyx-like patterns. The three on the left were found in Ghalekuti tomb I-V, Dailaman.

51

52

53. Rings and earring. Gilan Province. 1st–3rd century. Private collection, Tokyo.

The rings in the upper row are made of copper and have flat-surfaced glass settings decorated with human or animal motifs. The ring on the far left in the lower row is made entirely of glass, and the flat-surfaced setting is embellished with a piece of vermilion glass paste. The earring at the far right in the lower row is decorated with a round, dark blue bead.

54. Ring. Gilan Province. 1st–3rd century. Private collection, Tokyo.

A copper ring having a setting of light brown glass carved with what is thought to be a motif from Greco-Roman mythology.

55. Spinning whorls and miscellaneous objects. Gilan Province. 1st–3rd century. Private collection, Tokyo.

The pieces in the lower row are spinning whorls of blue, dark blue, or green glass. One is finished with a striped pattern made with white and dark blue glass strings.

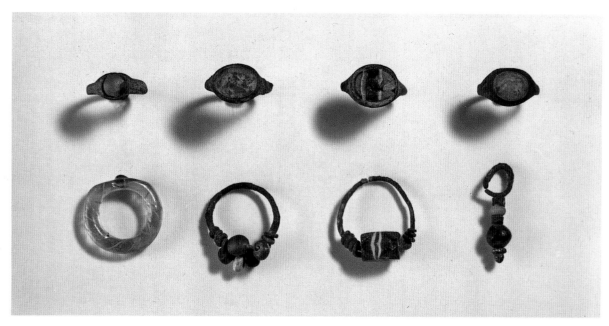

53

54

55

56. Charms and pendants. Gilan Province. 1st–3rd century. Private collection, Tokyo.

The flat beads in the lower row are "eyes" for warding off evil spirits and are pierced so that they can be strung. The pendants in the upper row represent a waterfowl and two dolphins.

57. Mask pendant. Gilan Province. 1st–3rd century. Depth .5 cm., diameter 1.5 cm. Private collection, Tokyo.

A pendant, designed like a mask, made of white translucent glass. The back is ground flat. It may have been set in a ring rather than used as a pendant.

58. Pendant. Gilan Province. 5th–7th century. Depth 1 cm., diameter 2.2 cm. Private collection, Tokyo.

A pendant depicting a hare. The colors used include red, dark blue, green, white, and gold.

59. Pendants and miscellaneous objects. Gilan Province. 1st–7th century. Private collection, Tokyo.

The four pendants in the upper row have mold-pressed designs of animals. The pendant second from the left in the lower row has a carved animal design and is known to be a work of the Parthian dynasty.

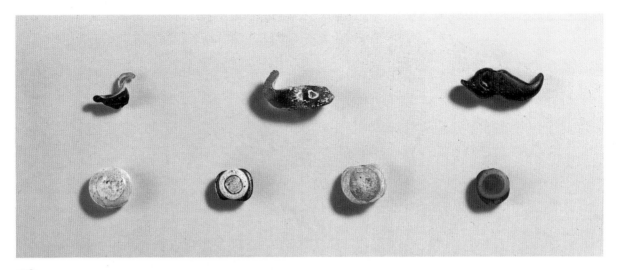

56

57

58

59

60. Bowl with incised decoration. Gurgan. 9th century. Height 5.8 cm., diameter 5.8 cm. Private collection, Tokyo.

A bowl of pale yellow glass, with an incised linear design on the body and an octagonal star cut into the base.

61. Bowl with raised almond-shaped pattern. Gurgan. 9th century. Height 7.4 cm., diameter 9.1 cm. Private collection, Osaka.

A bowl of white translucent glass that has effloresced. There are two horizontal rows of molded raised almond-shaped motifs, twelve in the upper row and eleven in the lower row. Both the exterior and the interior surfaces are molded.

60

61

62. Bowl with reticulated pattern. Gurgan. 11th–12th century. Height 9.5 cm., diameter 13.5 cm. Private collection, Tokyo.
   A bowl of dark blue glass with a molded reticulated pattern.

63. Footed glass bowl. Gurgan. 8th–9th century. Height 9.1 cm., diameter 10.6 cm. Private collection, Osaka.
   A footed bowl of milky white glass that has effloresced. The vessel bears both incised linear decorations and molded scroll designs.

62

63

64. Pitcher. Gurgan. 9th–11th century. Height 21.9 cm. Private collection, Tokyo.

A pitcher free-blown of thick light brown glass. The neck is embellished with trailed glass strings. The horizontal black line on the lower part of the body is not an applied pattern: that section is folded in like a pleat, and the thickness of the fold has caused the area to darken. The foot was blown together with the body. The beautiful curved line from the neck to the body is characteristic of pitchers of the early Islamic period.

64

65. Pitcher. Gurgan. 11th century. Height 13.4 cm. Private collection, Osaka.
A pitcher free-blown of dark blue glass.

66. Pitcher. Gurgan. 9th–10th century. Height 12.8 cm. Private collection, Osaka.
A pitcher free-blown of thin light brown glass. The shape of the handle shows the influence of the Sassanian style.

65

66

67. Bottle with handle. Gurgan. 12th–13th century. Height 14.8 cm. Private collection, Osaka.

Two areas of the long, thick neck are decorated with trailed glass strings. Two glass rings are attached to the neck.

67

68. Wide-mouthed pitcher. Gurgan. 9th century. Height 16.6 cm. Private collection, Tokyo.

The flaring neck is unique to the early Islamic period. The glass is thick, and there is a pontil mark on the base.

68

69. Wide-mouthed pitcher. Gurgan. 9th century. Height 14.2 cm. Private collection, Tokyo.

Three areas of the neck bear elongated facets and incised arcs. The body is divided into three sections, with four rows of shallow circular facets in each. There are incised lines and circular facets on the lower part of the handle and on the body just below where the handle is attached (see fig. 72).

69

70. Wide-mouthed pitcher. Gurgan. 9th century. Height 16.7 cm. Collection of Okayama Gakuen, Okayama.

The upper half of this vessel is made of dark blue glass, the lower half of pale yellow glass. Molded circular medallions decorate the body.

70

71. Long-necked bottle with cut decoration. Iranian highlands. 9th century. Height 16.2 cm. Collection of Tenri Museum.

A bottle of thick pale blue glass. The upper half of the tall neck is hexagonal; the lower half has two rows of six concave circular facets each. There are several rows of large concave circular facets on the body. This Islamic-period vessel is a splendidly crafted work showing traces of Sassanian influence.

71

72. Long-necked bottle with cut decoration. Gurgan. 9th–10th century. Height 21.6 cm. Private collection, Osaka.

An ointment bottle of white glass, having a shape unique to the Islamic period. The neck has planed parallelogram-shaped facets, and the body is decorated with an incised design.

73. Long-necked bottle with molded double facets. Iranian highlands. 10th century. Height 17 cm. Private collection, Tokyo.

A bottle of pale blue glass. The upper portion of the neck is decorated with trailed glass strings. The body is divided into six sections, each with a molded, double circular facet.

73

72

74. Long-necked bottle with tortoise-shell pattern. Gurgan. 10th–11th century. Height 23.8 cm. Private collection, Okayama.

A rare type of bottle, made of dark blue glass. The base of the neck is decorated with trailed glass strings, and the body is covered with a molded tortoise-shell pattern.

75. Long-necked bottle with reticulated pattern. Iranian highlands. 11th century. Height 23.2 cm. Collection of Okayama Gakuen, Okayama.

An ointment bottle of brown glass. In addition to the trailed strings at the base of the neck, the entire body is decorated with a molded reticulated pattern.

74

75

76. Ointment bottles with trailed glass strings. Gurgan. 11th–12th century. Left: height 15.2 cm. Center: height 10.8 cm. Right: height 13.8 cm. Private collection, Tokyo.

All three bottles are made of light brown glass and are decorated with strings of light brown and bluish green glass trailed around the neck and the body.

76

77. Ointment bottle with facets. Iranian highlands. 10th century. Height
9.9 cm. Private collection, Tokyo.
   A bottle of pale blue translucent glass. The neck is planed to a hexagonal shape, and the body bears cut decorations of a type unique to the
Islamic period.

78. Ointment bottle with facets. Iranian highlands. 10th century. Height
14.3 cm. Private collection, Okayama.
   A slender ointment bottle of dark green glass. The neck is hexagonal.
There are nine small circular facets on the shoulder, and eight vertical
parallelogram-shaped facets on the body.

77

78

79. Small jar with facets. Iranian highlands. 8th–10th century. Height 7.8 cm. Private collection, Osaka.

A jar of dark blue glass, the rim section decorated with seven facets. On the body are three rows of small concave oval facets.

80. Small jar with facets. Gurgan. 8th–10th century. Height 8 cm. Private collection, Tokyo.

A jar of white translucent glass. There are seven planed rectangular facets below the rim, which is decorated with silver, and two rows of large concave circular facets on the body.

79

80

81. Small bowl (left) and ointment bottle (right). Gurgan. 9th century. Left: height 2.6 cm., diameter 4.6 cm. Right: height 7.2 cm. Collection of Okayama Gakuen, Okayama.

The bowl has feathered decoration. The ointment bottle is made of green glass that has effloresced to a golden color, and bears applied ornamentation.

82. Vase with applied patterns. Iranian highlands. 9th century. Height 9 cm. Private collection, Tokyo.

A vase of brown glass that has effloresced to gray. The body is decorated with applied patterns.

81

82

83. Covered container. Iranian highlands. 8th–9th century. Height 7.3 cm., diameter 7.1 cm. Private collection, Tokyo.

A container of green glass. The lid is decorated with five facets, and the knob has a hole in the center. The body of the container is divided into six equal sections, each decorated with a double circular facet.

83

84. Bottle. Isfahan. 18th century. Height 31.8 cm. Private collection, Tokyo.
   A bottle of pale green translucent glass containing many air bubbles.

85. Ointment bottle with four handles. Shiraz. 18th–19th century. Height 26.4 cm. Private collection, Tokyo.
   An ointment bottle of thick dark blue glass.

84

85

86. Sprinkler. Shiraz. 18th–19th century. Height 17.6 cm. Private collection, Tokyo.

A sprinkler of dark blue glass. The tip of the long narrow spout has a bowlike decoration.

86

87. Stemmed goblet with floral pattern. Shiraz. 18th century. Height 18 cm. Private collection, Tokyo.

A goblet with enameled circular and floral patterns of gold, vermilion, and white on a dark blue enameled background.

88. Sprinkler. Shiraz. 18th–19th century. Height 25.9 cm. Private collection, Tokyo.

An unusually shaped vessel of dark blue glass, thought to have been used to sprinkle rose water.

87   88

89. Bird. Gurgan. 10th–11th century. Height 6.8 cm. Private collection, Tokyo.

The body and tail of the bird are made of clear glass; the comb, eyes, and beak of blue glass; and the breast, wings, and base of green glass.

89

The "weathermark" identifies this book as a production of John Weatherhill, Inc., publishers of fine books on Asia and the Pacific. Supervising editor: Suzanne Trumbull. Book design and typography: Meredith Weatherby. Layout of text illustrations: Suzanne Trumbull. Production supervisor: Mitsuo Okado. Composition: Samhwa, Seoul. Color platemaking and printing: Nissha, Kyoto. Monochrome plate-making and printing: Kinmei, Tokyo. Binding: Okamoto, Tokyo. The typeface used is Monotype Perpetua, with hand-set Perpetua for display.